BE STILL
AND KNOW

"Until one is committed there is hesitancy, the chance to draw back, always ineffectiveness. Concerning all acts of initiative (and creation), there is one elementary truth - the ignorance of which kills countless ideas and splendid plans: that the moment one definitely commits oneself, then Providence moves, too. All sorts of things occur to help one that would never otherwise have occurred. A whole stream of events issues from the decision raising in one's favor all manner of unforeseen incidents and meetings and material assistance which no man could have dreamed would have come his way."

— W.H. Murray

"Whatever you do, or dream you can, begin it. Boldness has genius, power and magic in it."

— Goethe

BE STILL
AND KNOW

MARA MARIN

DeVorss Publications

Be Still and Know
Copyright ©2006 by Mara Marin

ISBN: 087516823X
ISBN-13: 9780875168234
Library of Congress Control Number: 2006921864

FIRST DEVORSS EDITION, 2006

DeVorss & Company, Publisher
P.O. Box 1389
Camarillo CA 93011-1389
w w w . d e v o r s s . c o m

Printed in the United States of America

TABLE OF CONTENTS

INTRODUCTION

Kailua, Hawaii

I hope you dig into this book with great fervor. Something delicious is inside. If you are hungry, you will be well fed for it is written in that same spirit that prompted Job to exclaim, "Oh, that my words were now written! oh that they were printed in a book!" [1]

When you meet God, you change. In a "holy instant" your life comes into focus just as the dial of a binocular brings an unfocused scene into visual perfection. The thrill is so grand, the understanding so deep, the gratitude so immense that you are impelled to share, for sharing is the fate of all good things in life. Suddenly you wish to do unto others because something miraculous has been done unto you.

This little book is offered to remind you that you, too, have a date with destiny. Your past has brought you to this very moment. Go forth now on your spiritual journey. Your own "holy instant" awaits you. Along the way you will not be alone. "And, behold I am with thee, and will keep thee in all places wither thou goest ..." [2]

As you travel, you will encounter many dark nights, many deep holes, many tight spots. Sometimes you will feel afraid. Often you will become confused. At times you will wish to turn back. Do not be too hard on yourself. You are walking in new territory with an unfamiliar map. You are being asked to disregard familiar landmarks, to ignore your present instincts, to follow a strange voice to an unknown place. Have just a little faith for now. You will discover that there is a Helping Hand just ahead, waiting to draw you across the crooked places.

1 Job 19:23   2 Genesis 28:15

BE STILL
AND KNOW

A STRING
OF PEARLS

BOOK I

TABLE OF CONTENTS

THE INVITATION

The spiritual journey is a journey like no other. Although there is a destination, its direction is not from here to there but from without to within.

For this journey you procure your passport with commitment rather than cash. Your travel date does not appear on a calendar.

The spiritual journey does not require a change in lifestyle but a change in perspective. It inspires one to become receptive to soul spun revelation. The voyage will introduce you to truths about yourself that are beyond your current knowledge.

Deep inside you there is a voice that has been calling you for a long time. You have heard this voice but it speaks softly and disappears in the din of daily life. Its ever present echo lingers, however, waiting patiently for recognition. If you permit it to speak, it will reveal all that you have longed to know. It will fill you with renewed hope in everything you hold dear.

It is time to travel. Follow Me. The pearls are tender and are waiting to bestow their blessings on those who would receive them.

1 *If Ye Do As I Say ... Then I Am Bound*

Be still. Listen deeply. This is how you acknowledge God. All that you want awaits you. All that you need will be given you. Be still. Listen deeply. God speaks "in a still small voice."

In the beginning God created heaven and earth. And You. As you open your eyes, see the new day that is being offered you. Wake to the promise that it holds. Leave behind yesterday's life, last night's dreams. Resist the old self that you have made and invite the Self that the Lord has made to live this day. Your old self can do no right. It tries your soul, makes you weary and causes tears. The Lord can do no wrong. As your God-made eyes behold this day you will see with the eyes of understanding; as you listen with your God-made ears you will hear the truth. "If ye abide in me, and my words abide in you, ye shall ask what ye will, and it shall be done unto you."

How will your God-made self begin the day, live the day, rest at day's end? How do you "abide in me" and have his words "abide in You?" In wisdom. In simple truth.

In simple truth you will find an answer for any question, a solution for any problem, a resolution for any conflict. Truth is the only thing that is always true. It is a mighty touchstone. The sound of truth is precise. As you fine tune yourself you will recognize false notes in others; you will hear that which is insincere, self-serving, deceitful. Be still. Patience reveals truth, judgment does not. In any situation, let that which is true come forth of its own accord. Untruth falls away by lack of its own merit; you need not push the river, it flows by itself. When truth is revealed it will be as music to your ears, as a concert to your soul.

The light of truth is also precise. It will guide you in every delicate situation. Truth serves only itself. You will learn to recognize its traits. It does not compare. It does not discriminate. It does not pit one against another. It does not justify. It does not point a finger. It does not explain away. It does not defend. It does not complicate. It does not bewilder. It cannot hide. It is always just. It sets you free.

If doubts remain even when truth has spoken, it is time for silence. It is time to be still and to listen. "Prayer is not what goes from the individual to God -but that which comes from God, ... to the individual consciousness. Prayer is the Word of God which comes to you in Silence." [1]

When the Word comes you will know. Not one shred of doubt will linger. You will feel a wonderful release and a deep peace. You will know the simple truth. You will know who is telling it, who is not, what steps to take and what words to speak.

As you become receptive and responsive to inner direction, all difficulty unravels and falls away. Grace performs gently but speaks loudly. It is truth's messenger. Its demonstration in your life will extend to touch all who are ripe to witness it. Thus does truth never change yet ever spread. Thus does truth reveal itself to you and through you.

The patience with which you wait for truth to reveal itself is a distinct spiritual characteristic, that, once developed, will change your life. When you do not draw your sword in response to another drawing his, regardless of the provocation, you inherit the kingdom and may choose among its many mansions.

The Lord is always clear on what he would have you do; if your own consciousness does not offer moment by moment revelation, turn to those whom he has schooled as messengers. There are many who have gone before you who live by spirit and communicate in its language fluently.

As you hear the inner and outer voices of wisdom and embrace them with your understanding and acknowledge them by your actions, you are walking holy ground. You are drawing nigh to God and therefore He will make his Presence felt. Keep your promises to the Lord and he will keep his promises to you. If ye do as I say ... then am I bound.

2 "... And It Shall Come To Pass"

The spiritual journey is a quest. The search begins in each person's life at a particular time. Anyone who has already begun can pinpoint when their call came. It came when the going was rough.

In the symphony of time, pain is the lowest note. Expectations get frustrated, hopes get dashed, dreams get lost. It is an irony that one looks to the highest when one feels the lowest.

It is more ironic that suffering must become insufferable before one becomes spiritually receptive. Simple problems do not lead the way. Simple problems cause doubt, depression and despair but they do not lead to another world because one still feels control in and of the old one.

The spiritual life begins when darkness is the only color one can perceive. It begins when everything feels futile. It begins when the least disruption throws one into disorientation; nothing feels normal, familiar, worthwhile. It begins when one feels helpless. It begins with a cry, "Oh, God, help me."

It continues when helpless feelings remain long after the problems that seemed to cause them are gone. It is a journey which begins when one realizes that there must be more because what there is is not enough. It is a journey which continues when one can no longer stand the sense of separation.

It is in barren fields that soil may be made fertile. The Lord recognizes a barren field when He hears the cry for help. And He comes running. Is your door open or have you called out His name in vain? This may or may not be the moment that you choose to acknowledge an invitation you yourself have sent.

Time is an ever present moment. If you do not wish to wait upon the Lord in this one, it is only a matter of time until the next one. The Lord is available the very instant you decide to open the door in welcome. When you recognize your moment and definitely commit, Providence will bring you seeds to plant in your barren field.

Seeds are a precious gift. You who receive them must recognize and nurture them for in them is precious life, new life. In them is Your life. Leave behind the world of your own making where you misplaced yourself, and open to a world where God will feed you with daily bread leavened by your own faith.

With your tears and supplication you have asked for something more meaningful and you are receiving.

Plant your seeds in deep gratitude and with all your heart for they will bloom with the memory of who you really are.

In the symphony of time, grace is the highest note.

3 ... *In All Thy Ways*

The spiritual life is a sacred journey to a holy place. You must find your own path on which to take this journey because only your own footsteps will lead to where you're going. You cannot prepare for this journey. You cannot load up on provisions. You must simply proceed.

As you travel you will stumble and fall many times. There are unexpected challenges along the way. You may wish to turn back and, indeed, many pilgrims do. If you go forward, however, the rewards are so great that life lived in any other way is incomprehensible.

It is true that those who turn back seem to be spared. They eat and drink freely and appear to be merry. It is only an appearance. The food they eat will stuff them but not fill them; their drink will quench their thirst but not for long. Their merriment will fade to grogginess and they will fall deeply asleep. They will miss the real feast.

You may become hesitant when you see others fall by the wayside. Proceed anyway. Hesitancy is merely a simple test, one you can easily pass. You will come to recognize it as a simple vibration of fear that takes temporary occupancy in your physical self. It is unreal. As it passes you will be more sure footed for " ... they that wait upon the Lord shall renew their strength; they shall mount up with winds as eagles; they shall run, and not be weary; and they shall walk, and not faint."[1] When hesitancy strikes once again, you will recognize its powerless power. Such is the sweet taste of spiritual fruit.

New companions will now manifest. They will appear as interesting thoughts, new ideas, fresh motivation. Your days will be filled with stunning beauty and prayed for revelation. Each day will beget the next in satisfaction. When you lie down you will rest deeply. When you arise it will be with fresh inspiration.

Soon, however, the clarity will disappear and, once again, you will feel lost and forlorn. Yesterday's manna has been harvested and you are hungry again. That is why the path of a spiritual journey rarely moves in a straight line. It is more like a dance, two steps forward, one step back.

If viewed from a narrow perspective, the backward step makes you feel like a failure, like a groggy pilgrim. A more informed perspective is that the step back is the important one. It is here you see if you are on course and have gained ground or if you are going in circles. Here, more importantly, is where you gain momentum for the next step.

Doubt is an example of a backward step. While unpleasant, it is precisely the feeling you need to reconfirm your commitment. Unfamiliar territory is unfamiliar because you cannot use a map created by someone else's journey. When you are lost, doubt compels you to double check your bearings and to make sure you are following the correct Guide. Once assured, doubt transforms itself into confidence. You have not lost ground. You have gained higher ground. And tastier fruit.

11

A feeling of loneliness is another example of one step back. Fellow seekers have returned to worldly consciousness. You are not alone, however. Your Guide is with you. You are perfectly loved and cared for. " ... I will be with thee; I will not fail thee, nor forsake thee."[2] Your companions were only an illusion; they disappeared when truth appeared. Now that the illusion is dispelled, the crooked road will straighten.

Still another example of the backward step is a sense that you have too far to go to get there before dark. Where you are going is not a physical destination but a spiritual one and therefore the distance is covered by miracles, not by miles, by blessings, not by blisters. You cannot run out of light. The sun, the moon and the stars were created just for you.

Another feeling experienced in a back step is the fear that you are too old, too weary, too set in your ways to continue. Take heart. He art. Time, in its infinite wisdom, will carry you where you are going.

One last hesitancy that takes place in the back step is the fear that resources to complete the journey are scarce. This is unfounded. There are no provisions on this journey. What is scarce is faith. It will help if you remember that:

There is but one elementary truth ... that the minute one definitely commits oneself, Providence moves, too. All sorts of things occur to help one, that would never otherwise have occurred. A whole stream of events issues from the decision, raising in one's favor all manner of unforeseen incidents and meetings and material assistance which no one could have dreamt would have come their way. [3]

As you resume your journey once again, you see that each back step provided you with an opportunity to surrender yet another piece of your old consciousness. As you lightened your mortal load, you gained momentum for the forward stride. From here on you will recognize that God is your constant. His company will be your sufficiency in all things.

4 *The Secret Place of The Most High*

The spiritual journey is an experience. Although it appears to be a path that starts here and ends there, in actuality there are no footsteps at all.

In our day to day state of mind, our consciousness, we are aware of things on a moment to moment basis based on our perceptions. At times, we become aware of new things but they still occur to us from the way we ordinarily think. There comes a time, however, when our old perceptions fail to satisfy us. Certain ideas we've had no longer seem viable. Beliefs we've held dear lose their substance. Cherished truths we've lived by reveal themselves to be illusions.

As the old no longer satisfies us, we become anxious to know where else we may place our faith. This is the beginning of a spiritual journey.

Certain things occur to make you realize that a change is taking place. One day a coincidence might happen that doesn't even raise an eyebrow. The next day a coincidence happens and you recognize the hand of God. From this moment on, you are cast into the role of a seeker, ever looking for the secret place of the most high. It is important, first of all, to know that it is not found in the mind. Overcoming the illusionary power of thoughts is a spiritual demand that must be met before one is welcomed to further revelation.

Somewhere along time's passage, man forgot God and accorded the mind supreme power. Science was assigned the role of underwriter. Taught that we should live by its truths because they could be proven by this almighty discipline, we came to respect and revere great minds and deep thinkers. We believed that we knew God because we could contemplate him with our minds.

The mystical truth is that mind is neither the author nor possessor of knowledge. It is a receiving instrument with no dominion of its own. Mind is subservient to spirit which informs it. Understood correctly, it exists to receive impressions and impartations from spirit so that the children of God may live by direct revelation.

In the third dimension, which believes that the five senses report truth, everything is subject to the law of cause and effect. Things must be provable, repeatable, predictable or they are discounted. Thus, mind thinks itself to us resting on the fickle back of science which is only as accurate as its most recent tool of measurement. When yesterday's truths are rendered invalid, it covers its tracks with words such as progress, time marches on, evolution. In the timeless world of God, the world was never flat.

Truth is not subject to change. Truth is. God is its creator, its cause, the same as. The experience of this truth is provable, predictable, repeatable and will stand the test of all time. Those still in the third dimension, however, who believe mind is the knower, don't have access to this information because it is only discerned spiritually.

Where, therefore, does one begin to look when one has met the spiritual demand of releasing the mind of its attraction to illusion and its effects? One starts looking to this very day.

In the day's subtleties the reality of spirit is hidden. To those with wisdom's eyes, the subtle will be obvious. The spiritual aspirant, however, must develop the tools of spiritual perception in order for the hidden to be revealed. It is the job of a seeker, therefore, to learn what it means to have spiritual sight. An "ah ha" experience is a good preview. Two thoughts that were not connected, suddenly appear in relationship to each other and produce a new thought. The new thought causes one to see something in a new light, to understand something in a new way.

"Ah ha" experiences help us realize that outside the perimeters of the mind, which sees what it wishes, is the beginning of attaining correct vision in which we spiritually perceive. At this moment, truth makes its appearance because spiritual perception and truth are eternally mated and yearn, one for the other.

We can glance back now and "see" the suffering that our former misperceptions wrought. We can understand that our old lives no longer satisfied us because we were using mind as the knower and therefore "Ever learning and never able to come to the knowledge of the truth." [1]

The birth of spiritual eyes brings "insight" It brings the hidden into sight. The secret places are no longer secret. They shine with a light that spiritual eyes perceive. "... the Lord is in this place; and I knew it not." [2]

15

This place, which is no longer secret, no longer hidden, no longer somewhere else in space or in time is you.

Where else could the secret place of the most high be? Where else but you was the journey leading?

Within you now, therefore, recognize the pearls which have been waiting to dawn in your consciousness, waiting patiently for your welcome. String them together and you will see that the kingdom is at hand ... a prodigal has returned.

5 *The Lord is My Shepherd*

How do you know if your attempt at living a spiritual life is working? You'll know. The spiritual life is the natural order of things. It engenders peace, not problems. It creates prosperity, not poverty. It instills faith, not fear. You feel a definite sense of safety, correctness and confidence as you proceed in your day. You have a good morning, a good afternoon, a good evening because you experience the presence of a god morning, a god afternoon, a god evening.

Everywhere there will be signs that you are not walking alone but with spirit. The Lord offers little miracles throughout the day to give you bearings. They become like mini road maps that reveal the high road at every fork.

Learning to recognize the signs is based on your willingness to become aware of their presence. They take many forms and, therefore, the more you become receptive, the more you receive. A coincidence is a sign. Things that happen in the "nick" of time are signs. Surprises are signs. Exceptions are signs. Inklings are signs. Sometimes even the obvious!

Learn to listen to impressions you get during the day. Highlight your intuitive moments. Information may come in big print or little print, via proclamation or whisper, by person or predicament. It may appear as something you find or something you lose; something you feel or something you think. Signs are omnipresent-if you miss one, the next one is right there. You cannot lose your way.

Recognizing signs is different than reading signs. Once you surrender your doubt and accept that the Lord does not leave you unattended, you not only recognize signs, you learn how to follow them. A sign that tells you which way the mountain is does not mean you climb the mountain. It means you know where the mountain is. Reading a sign tells you whether or not to climb the mountain.

Nothing in the entire world will give you more joy and satisfaction than reading and following the signs posted by the Lord. Your entire life will fill with meaning and purpose. It will become easier, more exciting, indeed, at times, simply thrilling.

Exchange your own will for His. When you don't know what to do, listen. When you don't know what to say, listen. The Lord is communicating. You'll know exactly what to do, exactly what to say. As a spiritual disciple, the discipline you've developed will now offer the rewards for which you have labored.

At times, you may not recognize a sign or know how to read it. At other times, signs will feel confusing or mutually exclusive. Even in these moments the spiritual seeker is given a place of refuge. It is called meditation.

Meditation has deep significance. In the long run, it is a shortcut to the divine messages which you are trying to decipher. Once received, understood and followed they produce abundant fruitage. Meditation is simple, basic and immediate. You need nothing. Everything is present in the decision to enter into it. It makes no difference how you sit, where you put your feet or what you do with your hands or your breath. Meditation is not something you do with your body, it's something you do with your heart.

In meditation you invite God to speak. You let him know that you are present and listening. Meditation is a prayer that brings peace and comfort. Come forth, Lord, that I might be wholly holy. Come forth, Lord, and be with me. I am longing to feel you here and now.

When you reach for God from your heart, you will feel His spirit and a gentle Voice that says, "I am here."

6 *Pray Without Ceasing*

Prayer is beyond the best of gifts. It is a dream realized. It is a saving grace, a sacred power. One may pray at any time for prayer is of the soul and the soul never sleeps.

The medium of prayer is silence. Once the call goes out, words are unnecessary. Silence will deliver it. The Lord will receive it. He knows what you want before you ask.

Remain in silence. Let time pass. Time stills restlessness, impatience and agitation. Although thoughts will keep thinking themselves and clamor for attention, pay them no mind. They will disappear for want of welcome. Remember that you have invited a Guest of your own choosing and it is His words and thoughts that you are seeking.

Continue to let time pass. Waves of agitation will continue while your doubting self battles but ultimately the waves will subside. Time, the master healer, is changing the tides. Slowly at first, but very surely, your vibration will submit peacefully. Ever so gently, as you continue to surrender, your inner receptivity will begin to respond. The tiny mustard seed, which is the tiniest of all seeds, grows under time's gentle guidance to become the biggest plant in the garden. When you become totally quiet, you will become aware of a sensation of deep stillness. It feels very sacred. You will begin to hear but not in sound. You will see though your eyes are closed. You will feel but not by touch. You will know but not by thought. You will be in direct communion with the Lord. Joy will come upon you. This is how the Lord answers your prayers. Inside your self, he quickens your spirit and you awake to the truth of your identity.

From this moment on you will no longer be the same for spirit will change your entire life. Spirit is consciousness and perceives only truth. The first truth, last and only truth is that you are a child of God and that in your very own consciousness is the Father you seek. He is ever near and has always been with you, waiting for your recognition, waiting for your call.

You will recognize your new life immediately. In your undertakings, "all manner of unforeseen incidents and meetings and material assistance"[1] will come your way. The Lord will bless you from sunrise to sundown, from sundown to sunrise. In every moment you will feel safe and free. If you fall prey to a doubt or fear, the Lord will correct the false appearance, dispel the illusion, or remove the wrong impression so that you may be comforted with truth. His ways are mysterious only to those who know him not. You, who are awake in spirit, are protected by his eternal presence, his infinite wisdom and his mighty power. Omnipresence. Omniscient. Omnipotence.

As you go forth in consciousness, in recognition of your identity as a child of God, you will recognize the never ending supply of the fruit of spirit. The highest road will appear. The direction to take will be revealed. The best course of action will become evident. The wisest choice will become obvious. The most effective means will become available. In places you visit, your confidence and kindness will inspire a welcome mat to be set before you. Always your plate will be full and a bed nearby. You will walk in grace, with grace, by grace.

Pray without ceasing and you will walk arm in arm with the Lord, your God, as your constant companion. Pray without ceasing and you will realize heaven on earth. Real eyes will reveal that the kingdom is at hand.

7 *Destination ... Destiny*

You have reached your destination which was to find your soul. It was lost as you tried to live in the world apart from God. You were destined to be reunited. Destiny was your destination.

You and your destiny have never been apart. It sent you on your journey, accompanied you on each of its steps and was there to greet and welcome you when you arrived. It has been a loyal companion. It did not desert you or forsake you when you resisted it. It waited faithfully while you completed your many detours and was patient with you as you mistook other destinies as your own. Ever so gently did it keep the lantern lit so you could find your way back when you gently awoke.

To destiny does soul pay sweet homage for through destiny does the soul, returned to consciousness, remember God for whom it has longed to return from the moment it sensed its separation. Now it is home. It recognizes and remembers. Safety envelops it. Peace heals it. Love nourishes it. Grace imbues it.

Now does the soul know great delight and merriment and jubilation. It beholds the glorious earth it has inherited and the kingdom to which it has been given the keys.

Oh, what a place! In the Lord's house blessings rain down in omnipresent holy drops until our tears of gratitude fall as freely. Thank you, Lord, for bringing us home, for offering us a room, indeed, a mansion to lay down our heads. Thank you, Lord, for the feast at your table, the finest wine, and the tastiest meat. Oh Lord, thank you most for the

21

biggest surprise of all. You have not only bestowed the purest water ... you have given us the well.

Who but the Lord could deliver the best gifts. He led us from a dead end road to the living word and gave us royal welcome to his heart. No longer do we suffer mortal illusions. In the Lord's house nothing veils the stark magnificence of truth. We feast on the fruits of faith's long vigil and know our God. We hear him and speak with him, we feel him and love him. We use time only to learn how Thy Will Be Done.

Glorious is this day for on this day all things are brought to our remembrance. Our identity is revealed. Our purpose is made clear. We have knocked and it has been opened unto us.

8 ... *And Now Come I to Thee*

"And all things are made new again."[1] Evolving from one consciousness to another is a goal we did not perceive at the beginning of our journey. When we set out, we were hungry and thirsty but we were guided to an external search in an outer world. We prayed in holy places, made pilgrimage to holy lands. We convened with fellow travelers, studied scriptures, read spiritual books and spent hours in contemplation and question. Little did we know.

Our commitment to finding truth had to resist pulls from the material world. At times we wavered. Ultimately it only strengthened our conviction. With our passport renewed in passion we wandered further. With strong will we met the doubts that surfaced along the way and overcame the weariness that sometimes threatened to hold up our mission. Always truth pushed us from behind and beckoned us forward.

We saw many seekers stop to drink from empty wells. Sadly we soldiered on alone. We ate from fruitless tress, swallowed bitter herbs, and drank from shallow waters. We knew only one thing. We must find God.

Evolving from one consciousness to another is a goal we could not have understood at the beginning of our journey but that is the mystical way. When we look now, we see the worn out world from which we weaned ourselves. We remember the limits that mortal reality placed before us, and which, by our refusal to observe, helped us find a pathway that those weaned before us had already tread. Gratefully, we acknowledge the markers they left, as now we must leave ours.

Mind was the hardest thing to overcome. Armed with the power of omnipotence which we, ourselves, charged it with, it won the battle before we knew there was one to fight. It pointed to war and called it peace making, it painted an illusionary reality and colored it with persuasive thoughts. We were convinced of its omniscience. Only the heart's wisdom and spirit's grace revealed the accurate context for the mind and its thoughts.

Looking back, we marvel at the thousand earthly lessons that became our spiritual "blessons."

If it were not for our families who fed us but left us famished, we would not now be feasting at the Lord's table. If it were not for the physicians who saw only after our flesh, we would not have discovered the Healer. If it were not for the priesthoods who promised salvation but passed empty bread baskets, we would not recognize that we are standing in eternity right now and will be forevermore.

The mystical way runs over yonder and meanders on low roads that end in bridges that lead to higher ground. As the mystic looks back over the spiritual geography he has traveled, he notices that along the way, it was always the narrow road that revealed the next step on his journey. As he takes the final one, he now understands the words that the Lord spoke to Moses, " ... put off thy shoes from thy feet, for the place whereon THOU standeth is holy ground." [2]

9 *The Promised Land*

To the north of the promised land is a boundary defined by truth. To the east is a boundary defined by light. To the south is a boundary defined by peace. To the west is a boundary defined by faith.

Bordered on all sides by a grant of grace from God, the promised land is a battle free zone. One needs, however, to gird one's loins against the ever present foe of mortal consciousness. This enemy is ever on the march to regain dominion in the prized real estate of the promised land which you have entered. In the long run, it will create its own demise but, in the meantime, it will forge a mighty campaign to overthrow your tenancy.

At all costs stay the high watch and exercise vigilance.

Although the promised land is realized only by Word and ceded only by deed, it may be made vulnerable by innocence.

The most potent weapon in the arsenal of mortal consciousness is illusion. Parading as ally, it masks its intent to usurp your sovereignty by making alluring promises. Step right up.

Make no mistake about this. Illusions can convince you that there is a land other than the promised land. Believe it not, for if you go to the place where the enemy points a finger, he will steal your inheritance. Many years, many lifetimes may pass before you regain what was already yours. Hold your consciousness with all your might. Hold it closely and treat it dearly.

You have made it to another world, a different realm beyond the senses. Appearances no longer have the power to deceive you. By faith and the grace of God you have been given eyes to see and ears to hear. Truth was held safely waiting to be revealed to you.

You must be very committed to resist the grip of the long arm of mortal consciousness for it will come around again and again in a never ending quest for your glory. As you rise higher and higher in consciousness, use the polished tools of discernment to dismantle illusions as they appear. Innocence and forgetfulness must be disavowed. Recognize and rely only on revelation. Your daily bread will be provided.

In the Promised Land you are in this world but not of it. Remain eternally vigilant so that you may dwell in the house of the Lord. Forever. With your loins girded against mortal consciousness, you are the blessed recipient of the earth and the fullness thereof.

10 *Living in the Promised Land*

Spirit directs your life in the promised land. Having placed the guards of vigilance at the high watch, you have become a free citizen of God's government.

The first sense you notice is lightness. Fear is a heavy weight and, once lifted, you actively experience the inner vibrancy that resonates within the body. You become aware that the very act of breathing becomes an experience of pleasure. Each inhale causes waves of energy to course through your cells. As you feel this energy you naturally breathe more slowly and more deeply. Each exhale is a grateful recognition of the experience. As time melts to allow this inhale/exhale exultation, you become very present and recognize the divine breath breathing your life. The joy in this recognition is beyond any perception or conception of pleasure previously held. Even as you return to daily activity and the unconscious act of breathing, you will remain in the realm of awareness. You have been lifted above fear for you know, for sure, that I live, yet not I, God liveth my life.

The next thing you notice in the promised land is that external reality appears as an illusion. As you take in manna with each inhale of a God-given breath, you recognize the kingdom centered within. As a result perception alters. There are no hostages to take. Those whom you are already holding hostage seem unworthy of the energy it takes to fuel the judgment you feel. Judgments therefore fall away. You forgive for you know that they know not.

Unjust laws that formerly provoked you appear irrelevant; the unjust cannot serve up justice. You no longer live in an unjust world. You are living in God's world, under His government. Only His laws apply.

As you overcome judgment and remove yourself from the power of unjust laws to hurt you, you will lose patience with those who tarry. Their excuses become transparent. They become as unreal as the external reality in which they live. For a moment there is sadness and loss. The next moment, however, reveals true brothers and sisters and the gleeful reunion removes all traces of mourning for yesterday's acquaintances.

As external reality and the system and people that support it become as naught and fade into the oblivion from whence they emerged, a final alchemy transpires. You recognize the unleavened bread fed you by a pagan god. He who has offered everlasting life in return for repentance at his altar has not even one lifetime to offer. His words of truth have been tainted by the price of admission for he has sold his own soul and now needs and seduces yours. You, however, have been saved by divine intervention and recognition.

As you shed the skin of fear, overcome the illusion of mortal consciousness and cast out false gods, you are enrolled as a welcomed member of the brotherhood and sisterhood of mystics. Your new life will be full of grace. And surprise.

11 *Mystical Unfoldment*

Membership in a spiritual brotherhood/sisterhood in mortal life means a gathering. It offers a place of worship to meet and greet, to pray and celebrate, to sing and share.

This is a beautiful possibility; it is, however, not the mystic's way. Although it is possible to attend any worship service to enjoy communal prayer, a mystic's spiritual life is lived intensely alone.

Mysticism is direct union with God. It is not a religion. It has no liturgy or scripture. It has no hymns or holidays, no buildings, books or bibles, no priests or prayer books. The mystic meets God in the privacy of solitude. In deep silence he listens. When he has surrendered totally, the sacred words of God are received. It is a holy moment. The mystic knows God through direct communion and personal revelation.

The life of a mystic unfolds before him. His morning meditation starts the day in such balance that he learns never to start the day without first inviting, waiting for and recognizing God's presence.

Unfoldment is a miraculous experience. It offers all the excitement and joy that mortal consciousness promises but never delivers. It never gets old, on the contrary, it delights with its never-ending newness. In the beginning ...

Deep inside you there is a voice that has been calling you for a long time. You have heard this voice but, although it speaks softly, it no longer disappears in the din of daily life. It speaks clearly and reveals to you all there is to know. It is ever present. It will fill you with renewed hope in everything you hold dear.

Praise the Lord. One who prays knows Who I Am and will wear about the neck a living string of pearls.

Peace be unto you ...

REFERENCES

Page 7   1 Lorraine Sinkler, The Journey of
Joel S. Goldsmith, Florida:
The Valor Foundation, 1992

Page 11   1 Isaiah 39:31

Page 12   2 Joshua 1:5

Page 12   3 W.H. Murray

Page 15   1 II Timothy 2:7

Page 15   2 Genesis 28:16

Page 20   1 W.H. Murray

Page 22   1 II Corinthians 5:17

Page 24   2 Exodus 3:52

I will wash mine hands in innocency: so will I compass thine altar, O Lord: That I may publish with the voice of thanksgiving, and tell of all thy wondrous works.

Psalms 26:6-7

The Lord is my light and my salvation; whom shall I fear? the Lord is the strength of my life; of whom shall I be afraid?

Psalms 27:1

A FREE AND EASY SPIRIT

BOOK II

TABLE OF CONTENTS

THE SABBATH

Hello, My Friends. It has become very clear that now is the time of remembrance. We must become quiet, still, attentive. The world appears to be spinning very fast, spun by those who have forgotten that God's orbit is not rotated by the hands of man.

Declare liberty from the material world which races to a recycled tomorrow and regards not the revelations born this day. The precious things of life are all about you now and materialize with every beat of your heart. Listen to its pulsing message, speaking to you of a free and easy spirit in a life everlasting. It may be realized, must be realized, at your signal.

Celebrate this day as a day of Sabbath, for Sabbath is not a time or place but an activity which restoreth the soul. This very day, He Who thought you into life will quench your hunger and thirst with bread and wine.

Life, life, life. It is better the second time around for when you awake in consciousness, doubt and fear evaporate; there is nothing to sustain them. Come out and greet the life for which you have been ready and reaching.

At the precise moment you commit, the Divine will touch you. Faith will activate your journey. Patience will maintain it. Surrender will accomplish it.

Heaven on earth is a living truth, and now, beloved child of God, it is yours to behold ...

1 *The Spiritual Life*

The spiritual life is a wonderful life. It is available to everyone — yet not everyone is available to it for it is not an easy life. It demands total commitment because it's finest fruit ripens, like aged cheese or fine wine, over time.

At first, a lonely soul falls to his knees and promises anything that will deliver him. His heart is not in it, nor his faith, only his suffering. He pleads and then simply waits it out. This is what he knows best, waiting it out. Waiting for a far away god to arrive to save him.

In a while, for a while, the sense of futility eases. Relieved, he rises from his knees, ships God back to his distant heaven, and wanders back to the futile existence of material life. And promptly forgets why he was on his knees. If asked, he might say he was under the weather for a while, but, thank goodness, everything is fine now. Thank you very much.

This is not the spiritual life at all. Life with God is not appealing to God in times of trouble. It's about a life in which trouble has a way of passing you by. It's not about spending one day a week with God but about allowing God to spend seven days a week with you.

It's about remembering who you are, how wonderful you are and why you're here. It's about discovering the truth of spirit and the spirit of truth.

If you are ready and receptive to open to a deeper life, a higher consciousness, come along. You have read a hundred books and a thousand words on truth. Now is the time to put them to the test.

And there is no doubt, you will be tested. As you begin the search for meaning, the coils of mortal reality will spring into action to entice you to stay where you are, as you are. Here come the big, shiny things. New things. Things you have wanted for a long time. More money. Bigger house. Luxury car. Exotic vacation. Designer clothes. Precious jewels. Lots of toys.

Material consciousness plays for high stakes. It won't let you off easily.

Now is the time to take hold of your soul, dear one. Grace does not compete, will not compete, to get your attention. You must come to it of your own free will.

2 *Stretch Forth Thy Hand*

One who lives a spiritual life wrestles. It is easy to lose faith time and again.

The commitment to stay the course becomes intense. One has become used to living by limitations. He has inherited the truths by which others live and made them his own. What they say, he says. What they think, he thinks. What they see, he sees. How they live, he lives. He is a member of a tightly knit group which weaves a reality out of information appearing to the senses. This reality is not reality at all, but a quilt woven together by the common thread of misperception. It is stitched by mere illusion. It will unravel in time.

In the meanwhile, mortal reality is accepted as the norm of daily life. It captures and holds its participants hostage under threat of rejection and exclusion. It creates itself as the standard bearer of truth, formulates a double standard for right and wrong, and instills fear into nonbelievers. Anyone who dares question is persecuted by thoughts that he is dimwitted if not delirious, ridiculous if not retarded, cowardly if not criminal.

It is time to rise above the judgment of self righteous society. You know that there is more than meets their eye. You must take the journey to find out what it is. You know that thinking does not make a thing so nor does ignoring a truth deny its veracity. Does anyone have more access to God than you do? Does anyone have the right to restrict your liberties in order to increase his own? Does your heart carry less life than your neighbor's or your mind less wisdom than the one who creates the test to measure it?

Although you already know the answers to these questions, it requires a thrust into a new understanding to learn to accept, embrace and live them. Trust and thrust. Relinquish citizenship in the old way of thinking which takes its pleasures from the short sighted material world only to leave you bereft and bewildered. Leave the world of man and stretch forth thy hand to the loving arms of the tree of life that appears in the sanctuary of God.

Enter Eden where truth is the norm for truth is the parent of justice and justice is the parent of peace. Where there is peace there is eternal life for no one is left to convince you are naked. Everyone is clothed in spirit.

3 *In the Beginning*

Recognizing little white lies is a good beginning to living in spirit. Little white lies become so intrinsic to behavior that one does not recognize that they have taken root there or that they obscure the very truth they are created to protect.

Diplomacy is an example of a little white lie. It does not contribute to peace, it postpones it. Something said indirectly, or withheld purposefully, patronizes and confuses. The result is deception. Truth is the only correct communication. It has all the traits of diplomacy but is more powerful and much kinder. Communication is only about truth in the first place. In the only place.

Judgment is a little white lie. It is not about another but a cover up to disguise a personal sense of lack. Look deeply within where you may perceive that you already possess that which you covet in your neighbor. Judgment merely creates a holier than thou attitude which blocks the vision of your own blessings. Gratitude, not covetousness, will uncover them and increase them. Love thy neighbor as thyself. He is only a mirror reflecting your own sought after, soon to be realized, dreams.

Material things are little white lies. Although they are not denied you, they do not come first. They are the added things that follow the presence of the I am in your life. When you set store by the material world, rather than the spiritual world, even that which you already have gained will ultimately be taken. There will always be someone bigger, stronger, or smarter to diminish yours in favor of his.

The rewards of the spiritual life are priceless because they may not be taken from you. They will meet you on your own highest terms. Material life cannot make this claim. It offers you little more than flickering moments of joy that will tumble down the mountain of little white lies and crumble into a bankrupt existence. Only the Lord sustains and maintains you.

There is nothing, no thing, that will hurt you as you release the world of illusions. Their sudden exposure will cause temporary fearfulness but you can handle it. This is when those books on truth pass the test. This is when those words of truth jump off the page to offer comfort. This is when others on the path come your way to assist you. This is when miracles occur and blessings descend. This is when you discover your soul.

"The Lord shall preserve thy going out and thy coming in from this time forth, and even for evermore." [1] Let God take gently hold of your outstretched hand and lead you straightaway to his kingdom. You will recognize the place and the feeling for it is your own destiny and has a vibration specific to you. It is your own spirit come forth to carry you home.

4 *The Map Is Not The Territory*

It is usual to be wary at the beginning of a journey. Surprise throws one off balance, turns excitement into hesitancy. It is not easy to surrender control. When you feel afraid, remember that you are not leading, you are following. God is right with you, right before you. "I will perfect that which concerneth thee." [2]

Life lived based on information received from the senses has given you a false map. That map is not the territory. When you get lost, it is because your eyes and ears misplace the location of the high road. Have the courage to Follow Me for in that courage you will discover your destiny.

Life can feel very empty. Pleasures occur often enough but leave in their wake a sense of void. This unpleasant feeling leads one to immediately seek the next pleasure. Restrain yourself from this repetitive cycle of pleasure seeking for it is exhausting, demoralizing, futile motion.

You will soon discover that that which you are seeking is seeking you. Deeper pleasures unfold to the patient, faithful heart. They appear from the invisible map of your soul, for the Lord leads you to them by a way ye know not of. Strengthen your resolve to meet the pressure of this brand new journey by recognizing some emotions that will assail you. The impulse to buy things will increase. The desire to return to the familiar atmosphere of yesterday will get strong. The good old days of meeting life with ready made habits, beliefs and opinions will start to sound very appealing. Even old fears will seem easier to live with than the energy required to overcome them.

Your longing for the predictability of your past and its empty pursuit of worldly pleasures can stop you, dead, in your tracks.

Don't turn back. Don't look back. Don't go back. You will feel relief for the briefest of moments but it is not welcomed relief. It gives rise to deep futility. The higher you rise in consciousness the deeper you fall when you see the false idols who have called you back.

5 *Change*

The spiritual life is an inheritance of heaven. It will fulfill you completely because it disables the automatic pilot who runs your life and drives you into a state of perpetual anxiety. It allows God to enter and show you how to live by intuition rather than instinct, by revelation rather than rote.

Make simple changes. Examine every decision with an eye to its excellence. Permit every action to take into account the spiritual range of consequences. Evaluate each thought for its level of faith. Search all communication for its decree of truth.

Time unfolds in a unique way in consciousness. It is not measured in seconds, minutes, hours, days, weeks, months, years, decades, centuries, millenniums. Those drawn to more fertile soil respond instantly. Change is set before them and they change. Give water to a drooping flower and it comes to life. Feed soul food to the hungry and they rise. Their hunger is such that when the call comes they lay down their old consciousness and cast their nets to the other side, to the upper room. Right now, this instant.

For those who are not ready to wake up and change, no amount of time will make a difference. Lifetimes are irrelevant. What they see today is what they believe today. And tomorrow. They have stopped growing. They have died and are here in name only. You know when you are speaking to one for whom time has stopped. To one who has forgotten Spirit. There is no light in the eye, no hope on the face, no passion in the voice, no excitement in the demeanor. It is life as usual. Come back tomorrow.

The challenges of the spiritual life must be met with receptivity, not passivity. An on again, off again approach is not spiritual living. In spiritual living there is no off again.

As you start moving toward the voice of the shepherd, resist temptations. Do not stop along the way to laze and play or become distracted by a dazzling array of false appearances. You will lose your bearings. It will get dark and you will forget where you were going. You will no longer hear the shepherd's voice and will forget how to get home. You will end up on the road to nowhere, unable to change directions.

Do not let yourself be that person you meet on the street, the dead one who doesn't know he died. Oh, Lazarus! Come forth.

You are a spirit. Hear the knock. Open and answer with all your heart. God will appear at your front door. He arrives only where He is welcomed. When He is welcomed. Without exception. "For since the beginning of the world men have not heard, nor the eye seen, O God, beside thee, what he hath prepared for him that waiteth for him." [1]

6 *Royal Truth*

Simply stated, spiritual life is synonymous with truth. When you speak, speak only truth. Let your heart inform you. It knows the truth precisely.

You are the vehicle, the carrier through which the light of truth conducts itself. Through you, today's truth meets tomorrow. Truth goes forward through those who speak in its name.

When you speak only truth you may rest in the knowledge that tomorrow will receive all the good things of today. You will bear witness to this for you will reap tomorrow what you sow today. Your own heaven on earth is realized in this way. When you let truth live your life, you awake to the daily bread which nourishes the soul.

We have been told that we should be as little children. Let it be so. Let us regain our innocence. We no longer need to hide. We need not appear to be brave for we will be brave. Truth gives us courage.

Opening to receive truth is the soul activity of life. Living up to it is the soul purpose of life. Let truth flow and circulate the sacred space of your body temple. It will clear out the dross that weights you down, change the vibration that creates fear, evacuate the old beliefs that cause grief and disease. You will hear a new song; truth sings out in revelation and you have become the receiver.

7 *Faith*

God is always in your corner, always working on your behalf. When you commit to God, it means you surrender your own will and learn to listen for His. The time in between is called Faith. Take its wonders into your day.

To live in faith, trust, truly trust in the Lord and then step out of the way. He will take every truth you speak and every kindness you show and knead them into life giving bread to feed you. Every last crumb will contain a taste of heaven. Your goodness will come back to you five thousand times for what is yours must come to you. Your best will be returned as your highest. Your faith will be returned infinitely justified.

Your are not in charge of any outcome, only the input. Surrender your life to God and go about your business. Let the rising of the dough take place in His oven. Change will be imperceptible but you will soon witness the intricate problems of your life effortlessly dissolve and burn away. You will witness the miraculous.

Resist temptation to interfere. Do not compete with God. He is the Father. You are the beloved child. He will do the work. He will not forsake you. Time will reveal this. Time exists only to reveal this.

8 *Divine Rebuke*

Shortcuts are meaningless in spiritual time. Every moment you try to save you have to relive. When a thing is not finished it comes around again. Only when perfected does it permit freedom and revelation.

Meet appearances with a discerning eye, a knowing ear. When you hear an untruth, correct it. You are a servant in the house of truth. You are charged with responding when your ears hear falsity. You must expose the counterfeit, unmask pretense and call fiction to task. You must turn away inequity when it appears at your door. You must clear out evil when it sullies the altar. You must. You must.

Can you do this? Yes. When you are sure that there is no mote left to remove from thine own eye, you may tell others to go and sin no more. By divine authority, not man's corrupt laws, you may overturn the tables of the moneychangers.

In spiritual time every moment is a promise of Divine merger and you are the active example of its consecration. Travel only on sacred ground. There are prizes but no privilege for those who choose otherwise. Walking in footprints set down before you by God will burst your very heart with joy and recognition. In your person, natural light will shine. Those unable to stand near it, by it, with it, will go away but they will not leave empty handed. Their glimpse of heaven will linger. Although they won't know what they have seen, they will know that you have found something highly valuable.

The search for meaning ends on the Lord's highway.

9 *Soul Full of Heart*

In everything that you do, give your heart time to reveal itself. Although its information flows freely, the mind resists it, insisting on its own power as a determinant of reality. This is the way it keeps control. Or thinks it does.

Do not confuse truth and illusion. The mind uses rational argument to persuade the innocent to see things its way. At the moment one begins to sense the deception, mind whips into action and pulls out its two most powerful weapons. Guilt and shame. The fear thus generated is enough to dissuade many a seeker from going forward.

It is time to awake to direct knowledge from the heart. It is a skill easily learned. With just a bit of faith and focus, it will shortly become a natural activity.

You will know what your heart says via vibration. It will be subtle at first. Having ignored it for so long, it will take time to detect its' signal. Practice. Listen. Open. Breathe. The fear of feeling will slowly subside and with a miraculous sound, you will hear its direct communication. Your very spirit will lay it gently at the doorstep of your receptive consciousness.

Once you learn how to live from your heart you will never again override its offering. The information may be unwelcome or inconvenient but in the long run, and in the short run, it will save you time. Only messages from the heart have the power to restore the memory of who you are and return you to Heaven, your only home here on earth.

As resistance to truth subsides and is slowly overcome, its deeper implications will be revealed. The Lord will direct you with signs and wonders. Each situation will reveal its own resolution. Options that were once obscure will become self evident. Your decisions will be easier to make, wiser in their choosing. You will note an increase in confidence. Your sense of control will return. Feelings which once frightened you will now fill you with deep peace and gratitude.

Life lived from the heart is a powerful life. It disarms the weapons of guilt and shame that have been used against you. Nothing prevails against the spirit. Nothing.

Spirit and heart are soul mates. Together they lift you higher and higher, always above the problem, always away from the trouble. You rise in consciousness with a free and easy spirit. You look out and there before your astonished eyes, you see a new world. Columbus' discovery will pale beside it.

10 *Rising in Consciousness*

Your unconscious will constantly seek a way to become conscious. It contains vital information which it is anxious to share with you. When you ignore it, oblivious to the impulses with which it calls, you live in doubt and fear. The unconscious you, still seeking your attention, finds other ways to reach you. This is where you may locate the source of anxiety, depression, illness and disease. They are all underwritten by fear. Overcome them with your recognition of truth. Freedom and healing take place in faith's mirror, in truth's grace.

As challenging as the spiritual life may be, it is infinitely easier and more intelligent to live by its principles than to be constantly battered by the never ending troubles that come from disregarding them.

Now is the time to dismantle barriers between your self and your Self. Heed the call of your spiritual impulses and act on their lead. Consciousness will allow accurate information to replace the outworn, outdated and inaccurate information that constantly sources unhappiness. The entire atmosphere will change, like opening a window slowly to let fresh air into a stuffy room.

The new energy brings with it powerful vitality. It circulates rapidly, clearing fear and all its residue from the crevices in which it has hidden. A vibration, new and wonderful, is born. It has found a place of welcome. No denial is left to block its expression.

Your Self has a whole, new life to offer you. It has eyes that see and ears that hear. Appearances crumble and the reality of the spiritual dimension appears. It is called life everlasting because in it consciousness prevails and consciousness never dies. It lives to reveal truth.

You, dear one, will be lifted up and quickened in Spirit. Unto you are revealed all things. In you God makes good His promise. Through you, He shows forth His handiwork. On you, He hangs His firmament.

11 *Live Out From Spirit*

Life begins, regardless of counting, when you allow spirit to take dominion over your body and mind. Having risen to the recognition of heaven on earth, your mortal self has returned to the ground floor, ashes to ashes. Its' persuasive attempt to imprison you has failed, utterly. It lay now, gone forever, for it never was. Like a mirage, it took on a temporary appearance. Now you are in the realm of God where you see the world of man was never real. You were born asleep. Now You are awake.

Glorious, this meat for which you were hungry. You are divinely fed. Nothing may assail you.

Filled with the spirit of the Lord, you must live out from that Spirit. In all you do, do with passion. If there is no passion, there is no life, no substance, no spirit. Dead. Do something different. Come forth. Awake, take a divine breath, live. You are spirit now, spirit, spirit, spirit. Let it move you. Let it find you a new labor. You need not wake to dust off ashes. You are awake. There are no more ashes.

When you speak, share. Not that someone fell off a ten foot ladder onto concrete but that he rose and went about the day's labor. When you share, reveal. Not that you lost your job but that you found your true calling in its place. When you reveal, praise. Not how you have prevailed but how the Lord has made His light to shine upon thee. When you praise, raise. Elevate. Celebrate. Shout.

"For I have seen God face to face, and my life is preserved."[1]

12 *This Is The Way, Walk Ye In*

All things come to pass — until they reach perfection. Although God's world is perfect, man takes his lessons in time and therefore must wait it out. He falls again and again, using youth and strong will to scale the heights but manages only to age and watch his hopes dwindle. This is the way of the world.

Time is not the healer of wounds unless you live in time. There is another way. In it you do not take your lessons in time and therefore there is nothing for which to wait. You live according to divine principle where time is replaced by truth. Any required healing is accomplished by spirit.

Let it become obvious, therefore, that you must come out from time which is, after all, only an illusion. Man created it to account for his separation from God. He filled it with all kinds of appearances, created a faculty of reason to make sense of it, and believed that what he created was good.

What man creates is not good. It contains only illusions and causes endless, useless falls, leaving him disabled to all but hopeless dreams.

Hope again. Hope is eternal for it is faith's front door. Although you didn't scale the heights up till now doesn't mean you won't scale them in five minutes. Simply relocate your sights.

Withdraw your vision from the appearances that you created and didn't recognize as only appearances. Look away. When you look back, look for the face of God. He will reveal himself. He is omnipresent, always present. You cannot be away from him.

As a drop of the ocean is the ocean, so are you to God. You are intrinsically and integrally a part of Him. There is no separation other than the one that your misperception created. You may only be disillusioned from the illusions in which you mistakenly placed your faith. You are not here and God there. He is ever with you. "For wither thou goest, I will go and where thou lodgest, I will lodge." [1]

We arrive back at where we started, perfection. In the beginning the Lord made the world and saw that it was good. Return to the light that never went out but only got dark as you moved away from it. As you placed yourself in time, you lost your faith in life everlasting. Welcome back. Your place is still here for it is your place. God holds it for you no matter how long you are away, be it hours or lifetimes.

Correctly perceive the mountain that causes you to stumble and fall and you will see that there is no mountain from which to fall. You have scaled the height. You are at the pinnacle, the place of the Most High. There is no other place. You could not see it before because your old consciousness could not perceive that you were already where you were going. There is no time in spiritual reality. There is only God and you and now. God, as you, always. He raised you up on mother's milk that you might one day drink His wine.

"Therefore the redeemed of the Lord shall return, and come with singing unto Zion; and everlasting joy shall be upon their head; they shall obtain gladness and joy; and sorrow and mourning shall flee away. I, even I, am he that comforteth you ..." [2]

13 *Call Upon Me And I Will Answer*

When you call upon the Lord and receive the answer, you begin to live. Never again do you seek the old garment to wear. You take on the purple robe of the seasoned traveler. The journey from rags to riches reveals the high road on which you now stand. You may not go higher but you may go deeper.

You are blessed. Your idle wanderings on roads that lead nowhere are left to those who are still lost — those who do not call upon the Lord for direction.

Your life is made new. Confidence will underwrite your consciousness. There is no concern for outcome for you have already received the answer. No matter how steep the problem, the resolution will become visible at your approach. All ongoing dilemmas that appear will dissolve — truth decides on behalf of those who honor it.

In every instance, remain in stance for revelation. Whatever the confusion or confounding, "Behold, the Lord God will come with strong hand, and his arm shall rule for him: behold, his reward is with him, and his work before him."[1]

Call upon the Lord. The moment you call, the answer will answer. It will be shot as an arrow, heading straight to your receptive consciousness. The call and the answer are One and the same. Marvel at this. The call is all you do. The very call is your very answer. Call, call, call. He will answer, answer, answer. Like an echo, echo, echo.

And the words that come forth from His mouth shall prosper in you and cloak you in a free and easy spirit. "And it shall come to pass, that before they call, I will answer; and while they are yet speaking, I will hear." [2]

14 *Prayer*

The way to call upon the Lord is through prayer. Prayer is a spiritual tranquilizer. Five committed minutes can undo a lifetime of doubt.

Prayer is a sitting down to listen in. Behind thousands of thoughts, there is truly a place of peace and poise.

The mind does not sanction this space. It tries to keep you thinking and worrying, to tumble you about in a chaotic jumble of overwhelming considerations. If you show ability to resist, it produces a bevy of anxiety provoking what ifs. It simply refuses to acknowledge defeat.

Prayer is a place of retreat where the mind tries to follow but cannot. The tide of spirit crashes it against still waters.

Now you may rest. In the deep retreat of silence, the heaviness created by useless thought lifts. Your vibration shifts. Information starts flowing from spirit, lighting up a clear path through the chaos and revealing, to your delight, that nothing is falling apart, nothing is out of order.

As your begin to experience hope, safety and well being, the deeper gemstones of prayer are unearthed and deliver profound understanding to your silent sanctuary. Little by little you begin to feel the Presence. This communion will alter you forever for you are at spirit's altar and it is revealing, to your immense relief and gratitude, that you have found Home.

Later, when you open your eyes, you won't believe how many clock minutes have ticked by. You will feel like you are returning from a far away land yet, there you are, right where you were when you started to pray.

The Lord, in his infinite wisdom, installed life in the temple. You are that temple and He is the Landlord Who lives within.

15 *A Free And Easy Spirit*

You will love your new life, full of calm and grace. It has taken its Sabbath. Your soul has been restored, recognized, sanctified.

The blanket of mortality has lifted, uncovering a world of simple blessings and holy moments.

Now you remember who you are. You are the finest fruit of the tree of life. When you fall to your knees it will not be to plead but to praise.

You have made your commitment and Providence has moved. All manner of unforeseen incidents, meetings and material assistance which you could not have dreamed of will come your way. Grace will scatter the troubles that appear on the horizon and they will drift away. You may go in peace.

You have been called and have answered yea, yea, yea. Yours is life everlastingly as a free and easy spirit.

"Arise, shine; for thy light is come, and the glory of the Lord is risen upon thee." [1]

So let it be written. So let it be done. You and your Father are eternally One.

REFERENCES

Page 40 1 Psalms 121:8

Page 41 2 Psalms 38:8   138: 8

Page 43 1 Isaiah: 64:4

Page 50 1 Genesis 32:30

Page 52 1 Ruth 1:16

Page 52 2 Isaiah 51:11-12

Page 53 1 Isaiah 40:10

Page 54 2 Isaiah 55:11

Page 56 1 Isaiah 60:1

"To everything there is a season, and a time to every purpose under the heaven."

Ecclesiastes 3:1

"Then shall ye call upon me, and ye shall go and pray unto me, and I will harken unto you. And ye shall seek me, and find me, when ye shall search for me with all your heart."

Jeremiah 29:12-13

THE SEASONS
OF SPIRIT

BOOK III

TABLE OF CONTENTS

THE TURNING

The seasons of spirit move like the seasons of earth. One gracefully unfolds unto the next until a cycle is complete and all things are brought forward, more evolved, more conscious, closer to God. Nature makes her rounds once a year. Spirit can cover the ground in just a day.

The winter, dark and dreary, happens at any time when you are struck with fear or overcome with doubt. Spring happens at the moment you get a peak beyond them. Summer is the moment of surrender when a Sabbath peace returns to restore your soul. Fall occurs when you're back in the saddle again, ready to ride with renewed confidence.

Sometimes winter is long and exceptionally cold. Sometimes grace lingers in a beautiful Indian summer. Nothing is set in stone, not even stone. The cycles of change are merely God's way to show the infinite array of possibilities so that we may be prepared, when our time comes, to recognize and embrace the emergence of our own spirit.

Things flow. They are urged tenderly by time until their immortal essence is revealed. God's hand reaches into time and space to touch everyone.

When your time comes, and it has already come, you will understand your sacred purpose under the heaven. The universe will sweep you into her grand design that you may carry out that which you are given to do. It will open the way and grant you unlimited resources so that you may carry out the Lord's will in concert with the everlasting cycle of life divine.

1 *Winter*

To everything there is a season. Even the spiritual life unfolds in divine order. Winter is as much a condition of the soul as a description of weather.

The spiritual life starts in the dead of winter. One leaves spirit out in the cold and forgets all about it. The grapes of wrath become stuck with frost. The water of life turns to ice. One's daily bread is snowed under. Doubt rains down hard and the seed of birth is buried deep. "And the earth was without form, and void; and darkness was upon the face of the deep." [1] Yet winter is the ripest time for development, not spring when the buds have already declared themselves.

Winter is the beginning when all things are being made new. It is the season of the dark nights of the soul. The wheat and the chaff are starting to separate, and the old ways will not make it though the stormy nights of change. It is the time that fear is desperately seeking warmth, hoping for the thaw that may render it safe.

Winter is the most vulnerable but spiritually receptive season. As man stays indoors to weather the storm, he is forced into vulnerability, a perfect place for the Lord to enter "for my strength is made perfect in weakness."[2]

And you will need the strength for it will fortify you for your upcoming renewal in the fertile soil of spring when you break the ground of frozen beliefs. Your past will let you go after this final winter fling. You'll emerge into the light, pushed by the Lord's will until your reluctance gives way unto the lilies of the field.

As you go from winter season to spring, you will travel from the belief in good and evil to the knowledge that God is preparing the field, pouring the rain and blowing the wind so that everything may come forth in due season. There is no good and evil. There is no good or evil. There is only God, doing God's work. Good and evil belong to man.

Winter is the time to peek behind every shadow, looking for the light source. It is the time to let the seed in the winter womb enjoy the nourishing hearth where you need do nothing but watch the Lord fertilizing his own. It is the time to face the discontents of your mortal mind and let your heart's desire plow through the piles of illusions that hold back your blessings.

Winter. Look around. It is dark and windy and cold and you are stuck inside, no where to go, biding time, praying amiss that winter will soon pass. Look again. The Lord's blanket of snow is as bright as any light. It draws the rays of the sun so it may melt in time to water the spring flowers and drench the reservoirs of man's spirit with renewed hope. It is preparing to soak up the illusions of material thought that have clutched him in confusion, depression and futility.

Winter is the gentleness of newly fallen snow bringing the stillness of peace so that the tender warmth of God's love can melt the chill of fear and the ice cold despair of doubt. There is no rushing about in winter. One is captured.

Winter is cold but it is only part of a cycle. It is only one season of a year. No sooner does it begin than thoughts of spring are not far behind. Winter is the way station to shiver for a moment and to come naked before the Lord that he might clothe us in the warmth of his purple robe of perfection. It is the time when we say, "Speak Lord, for thy servant heareth." [3] All is quiet and the ears are desperate to hear news

65

of the Lord's coming, of His grace and of His mercy.

Winter is the season when the nights are long and we sleep deeply to mourn and hide. We toss and turn in the maze of a hundred petty problems before the Lord comes to retrieve us from their grip and point us to the dawn's early light. "This is the way. Walk ye in it." [4]

The darkest hour is right before the dawn of understanding. It is the final moment in the womb before the birth of a new consciousness. Though it be the darkest hour it is merely the graceful way to let worldly thought and mortal reality come to nothing. It is the emptying of a time of error, of conditioned thought formed by the mass hysteria of man's fears collected up and deposited in man's unknowing psyche.

In the darkness, the Lord may work his wonders in the mysterious ways of silence, breaking up the unreal thought patterns that hold sway in consciousness until the bits and pieces of truth are allowed to escape the frigid ground of disbelief. One is made over in the image of his Maker. In the winter, while one is complaining of the bitter cold, the Lord is making the spring soil fertile and warm. One's cold heart has not far to go.

As winter comes again and again it will not be measured by life span but by how far we have come. The shadow of death gets lost in light.

A new dimension of ourselves is always preparing for our arrival.

Bless the winter. It is when the light of spirit becomes a lamp unto man's feet, the turning of the tide that crashes man's disbelief into revelation on the peaceful shore of truth.

The short days of the mortal life span are overturned and emerge into the long days of repose in the realm of consciousness.

Winter is the time when all that feels lost comes up for life review, creating an opportunity to do it anew, this time with more in sight, even as the April flowers don't bloom till May. It is a time that faith, dead on winter's cold vine, gets a peek at hope, a taste of patience.

Winter is the reality that the mind must surrender to the sure touch of the Lord's hand- helping us to see that we need no longer carry our burdens alone. In the winter of spirit we learn to call His name, to ask to be delivered to the promise of spring. We knock and open our ears and remain still so that we may hear His voice. It calls to those with eyes to see and ears to hear and tells us simply to follow our hearts. The Promised Land is a real place, a true promise. It is the only real place, the only true promise and the prisoner of a winter spirit will warm to the grace of the Lord's call and come out to see. Glorious and mysterious, how the bitter cold of winter can crack the ice of our entombed spirit so that it may escape and rise in consciousness.

Seek ye first the kingdom of heaven which starts in the winter when the darkness obscures the light and sets the traveler on his spiritual course. As he undresses his grievances and sees the thin ice on which he has lived his life, the whole world of truth waits to lift him to the elect of God. It takes courage but one will rise to it. There's no worthwhile thing to hold him back.

The prodigal son begins his journey in winter. Too long has he trekked on cold feet and ended up lost again and again. He is coming home. Yea, coming home, waking up, breaking the icicle of blindness and seeing the crooked road made straight in order to return him to his Father's house. He can feel his cold blood starting to simmer in the image and the substance of his maker and knows that he must pray without ceasing for he has been out in the cold for too long.

He has collided with mortal reality and collected trinkets that appeared to his human sense as gems. He has mistaken bits of colored paper for the green, green grass of home. He has combed the world for treasures and ended up in combat for his very soul. He is battle weary, fatigued with the endless cycle of an eye for an eye which has left him no sight at all. He has collaborated on the cold front of a godless reality and been knocked cold with hopelessness. He has forgotten his high estate.

So does the soldier return from the lost war, tattered, hung low, fighting the battle of good and evil to no avail for it was all an illusion. As he saw the enemy's eyes and tried to put them out he came to know that all men were his brothers and that all his brothers were God's children and he was stopped cold and could kill no more, regardless of who claimed authority for the command.

Thou cannot serve God's laws and man's laws. They are mutually exclusive. He must return to the Father's house which rules by wisdom, which requires only the recognition and activity of divine principles. The time we are given in this life is to learn and to live by these principles, no matter what temptation there is to lead us otherwise.

We must gain sight of the Lord our God for in His recognition lay our peace and prosperity. Life will plague us with fear and futility otherwise. "Sanctify yourselves therefore, and be ye holy: for I am the Lord your God. And ye shall keep my statues, and do them. I am the Lord which sanctify you." [5]

The prodigal has given false beliefs to everyone along the way in hope that they would shower him with love, bestow him with honor and fill his baskets with five thousand loaves. What he found is that what he sought he left at his Father's house. Return ye home.

You are not of this world any longer. You left heaven to eat meat that fed you not. Return with your hunger and you shall dine on a Sabbath feast fit for the son of a true king. Hear, oh Israel, God never slumbers, never sleeps, so that He might catch His prodigal out of the cold and give him warm welcome, "And I will give thee treasures of darkness, and hidden riches of secret places, that thou mayest know that I, the Lord, which call thee by thy name, am the God of Israel." [6]

Winter, winter, winter, we dread the thought but in essence it is a remarkable part of the journey and it comes upon us on behalf of our spiritual development. We might not take the steps that evolve us without it. It is a pregnancy that stores an immanent birth, both of spring and of spirit. We must prepare for it or we will literally be out in the cold. The preparation is what gives us faith that we will survive in the end regardless of the hell or the high water.

As we prepare to suffer winter we pile logs for the hearth, store extra grain, retrieve the umbrella and boots. We purchase tire chains, pay up the heating bills and buy candles by the score. Thus, as winter approaches, she finds us ready to receive her and to be as comfortable and safe as we can under any of her conditions.

In this preparation we have gone another level of consciousness. It is this level that rekindles the spiritual life. Prepare ye the way of the Lord. Do not be blinded by what you see now for the times they are a changing and you must make room for the things of the spirit. Your whole life is going to transform.

You no longer live in illusion once you give up your mortal perceptions in order to live by divine understanding, for divine understanding rains down in buckets into receptive consciousness. Your past is wiped from memory and your sins are made white as snow. As you live by truth you can see every pothole of mortal belief. In the bright light of newly fallen snow, you are gently cleansed of your ignorance and your vanity. As the snowflakes fall, your judgments disappear and your enemies disappear at the same exact instant.

As your illusions melt, they change to naught and the nourishing minerals of truth will replenish your spirit. You come through a whole new season, dripping away one misperception after another until you get to their very source. You save forty brutal winters in the desert of ignorance.

One by one, you cast off the errors until you see temptation itself playing with your mind, tempting you with a mirage a minute until you are blind and cannot see through its glass darkly. Your whole life has not been yours but cut up into a thousand pieces to pay off your guilt. You are left with nothing. No part of you is alive in the dead of winter. Even the log on the fire which gave a few hours warmth and glow is now turning into bitter embers.

As the light of one fire goes out, the light that never goes out comes on, the light of your soul. The things of earth may pass away but your soul is eternal and out of the ashes of the dying embers are shooting up the flames of life. Your vision is clearing. Your mind is emptying. All your false beliefs are straining their seams.

You are not alone. You have never been alone. You have merely forgotten who you are and who your Father is and where you are and why you're here. You have laid your soul to rest and forgotten where you laid it. As you went searching up a multitude of blind alleys, you forgot what it was you were searching for and gave up altogether. You accepted the world as your home.

You disappeared into the byways and highways of mortal reality that measured the man by appearance, bank account and the ability to sell ice in winter by a fast talking tongue. You sold out over and over, never doing your heart's desire but crouching under the whip of man's godless commands. Each act of trying to get something for nothing cost you a pound of flesh and a piece of your soul. Each shortcut to glory and riches landed you in yet another shallow grave where even your dead bones could find no warmth. Every lie you told a brother became another nail in the coffin of your freedom until you could no longer tell deceiver from deception.

You paid off every pied piper regardless of the dead meat they were selling as long as it looked good. You worked by the sweat of your brow but held back because your heart was not in it and therefore stole from your future. You cut corners that weren't yours to cut, took from others that which was not your due until you took yourself to the cleaners but could not clean up your mess.

But when winter comes, spring is also on her way. And the red robin of hope hops into view, eternal in the human breast. As you suffered the helpless Jobian cries of despair and wailed at God, suddenly you began to see where you mislaid your fortune and how you were trying to collect gold from man's glitter mine.

Ever so quietly, through the crack at the bottom of the door, there is a bit of light. Right there, piercing the veil, are the new sounds and new words, hearkening you to consider a brand new world. It is called heaven on earth and requires your utmost attention.

Winter is the doorway to the soul. It keeps the home fires burning that man may come in from the cold and out of the dark and behold the works that were beyond his reach. Winter's storms do pass. One comes to understand that the Lord works in mysterious ways to help man leave his dead tracks in the snow and head for higher ground. From this high ground we will hear very miraculous things.

We must come out of winter with the wisdom with which to understand these things for it is only as man that we cannot understand. With the eyes and ears of spirit, the Lord may come upon thee in full view that his praises may be sung and His glory revealed to the world. Be thou as one with eyes and ears of spirit for winter is indeed passing. The dark night of the soul is no longer bearable. It is time to turn the other cheek and be done with it.

Hear, oh Israel, the Lord my God has come for me and I am coming home. There in the distance do my new eyes see heaven. Before, it was only a mirage which led me astray down every path that man walked and I could see for naught. I am saved by my own right hand and I am awake. I have left the darkness which was bleak and merciless, filled with the pride and vanity of the self righteous. I have arrived to the garden's fertile soil all cleansed of man's illusions of treasure where there was none.

Now can I see the gated community that man called heaven as no heaven at all, just a place that man hoped he would weigh well in the balance and get a walk through. Oh, no, that is not God's heaven. That is a retirement community for man waiting to be divinely recycled in hopes that he might get it right the next time around.

God's heaven is on the other side of the dark night of the soul. It is the white shadow of spirit emanating from the light source within which no man can put out, even in the dark of winter.

2 *Spring*

Springtime is winter's payoff. The dark night of the soul, encumbered by a forty year mortgage to mortal reality, is paid in full and brings one the deed to the Promised Land.

Something in the breast stirs as the March lion meets the March lamb and a new vibration begins to rouse in the whole universe. Everything is still with intense excitement, like the silence that fills a large auditorium before the symphony breaks out in psalm. It is the moment that the soul's prayer for deliverance crashes the sound barrier and enters the ears that hear. God is here. Wake up, wake up. Spring has arrived. Every living thing begins to move. God is here. God is here. Spring time has sprung, flinging loose its cache of hope to feed the hungry. One's eyes feast on the seeds of grain as they leaven into five thousand loaves. The grapes of wrath have thawed and prepare to offer the sweetest of wines. Everywhere the green hint of renewal is peeping through, as if Lazarus were coming forth from the multitudes of all souls at the same instant.

Winter has passed. "For his anger endureth but a moment; in his favour is life; weeping may endure for a night but joy cometh in the morning."[1] Man has been so lonely that he believed that he was alone. He has been deeply afraid. Springtime releases him. The excitement is unmistakable. Man is spared. His salvation is fed by the pure water of winter's run off that prepares the way of the Lord, the way of love. Spring is in the air and man is breathing the pure inspiration of soul recognition. He is vibrant with renewal, sensing his birth into a new day where he will never feel alone again and never afraid. "But who so hearkeneth unto me shall dwell safely, and shall be quiet from fear of evil."[2]

And the March winds cometh and bring their mighty power to dust off and clean out the old idea and sweep up man into his joyful life, renewed in spirit, increased in understanding, deepened in recognition of the one and only God. It is spring. "And the glory of the Lord shall be revealed, and all flesh shall see it together; for the mouth of the Lord hath spoken it."[3]

Spirit is newly arrived into consciousness and its activity is bustling about, arraying the lilies of the field, opening the hearts of man and lifting itself into realization to those who have asked.

Spring is the Promised Land, the fertile soil for man's birth into the holy tabernacle where the words of the Lord endureth forever. Spring brings man to his spiritual senses, firing him into glorious revelation of his identity as a child of God. It brings flight to his prodigal feet and hurries him home for reunion with his Father.

Wake, wake. The Lord has come. Into your sleeping soul leap the flames of light that will burn off the dross of blindness and open your eyes to the God of Abraham, Isaac and Jacob, the God of Moses and Elijah and Jesus and Mohammed, the God of the Jews and the Christians and the Hindus and the Muslims and the Quakers and the Mormons and you and me and every life. Amen. Amen. Amen. "And God saw everything that he had made, and, behold, it was very good." [4]

And you are very good. And now is the time to recognize and accept your goodness, to see yourself in the mirror of spring. The old glass darkly is left behind, melted in the old winter of discontent. What you see is the reflected glory of the Holy Spirit in a thousand mirrors which do not break up the light but multiply it a thousand, thousand times. "Thou hast turned for me my mourning into dancing; thou has put off my sackcloth, and girded me with gladness; To thee and that my glory may sing praise to thee, and not be silent. Oh Lord my God, I will give thanks unto thee for ever." [5]

You are born again in spring, born to live forever, eternal in the heavens. The Lord is at your side, ever with thee, showing you the ways you missed the mark before, carrying you beyond your ignorance and into the ways that you should go. He has forgiven you everything. Your soul is white as snow, not a mark left to judge you or deter you from your walk with the Lord.

Onward, into the word made flesh do you carry forth in spring, no longer waylaid by a hundred detours in which mortal life and material thoughts detained you. You have been set free. Truth has declared her thunderous words into your temple. You are welcomed at the tree of life in the Garden of Eden where you may eat freely and forever.

Crops of joy and peace and love are growing in your garden. The seeds which you sowed are returning to you hardy and strong, feeding from the fertile soil of spring. They are growing mightily, quickened by spirit, to feed all God's children and to leave not a one hungry or thirsty, not a one lost or lonely, not a one in doubt or fear.

The Lord feeds his children, maintains them and sustains them and takes great pride and joy in giving to thine all that He hath. For any eleven who would come to his feast there are twelve baskets of treasure.

As you dwell in your Father's house and accept his gifts as your supply, you will eat handsomely while your brothers who are still in the trough of the world are foraging for their next meal. They cannot be satisfied. A dozen gifts at the birthday or two dozen at the holiday or one big one at the lottery do not fill their hunger for more, more, more. Oh, how they yearn to be filled, to be satisfied, to end the maddening turkey gobble and snap off the bigger piece of the wish bone, but it is not to be. They are not tilling in the fertile fields of the Lord and are coming up hungry. They are far from home. Perhaps next spring.

In the meanwhile, you must look for company only to those who seek God and wish to know Him aright. The others, still beholden to the ways of the world, must endure their own version of winter. You cannot do the work for them. You can only hold fast to your own ladder of consciousness.

Just at the sprouts of spring planting shoot up toward heaven and become food for the body, you must reach for the food that will nourish your own soul. You must seek your daily bread from the fields you have planted with the seeds of life, for you reap what you sow, day by day.

That which is not yours cannot come to you and if, perchance, it does, return it. It will only toss you overboard and leave you drowning in a sea of doubt. That was winter's work. In spring you glory with the leaves that are appearing on the twigs and the branches. Your eyes get bigger and your ears hear more for there is so much color to see as the roses bloom and the pansies play and the lilac bursts into fragrance and the golden mustard seed creeps across whole fields in one blink of spring's eye. All for you. For if it is not God's pleasure to give you the kingdom, for whom does he dress those fields with food and flowers. For whom does he create the sights and sounds of birds singing, children laughing, lovers meeting, rainbows forming, consciousness materializing. For you. There is none other.

He brought you as slaves from the barren land of Egypt that you might become beholders. Therefore, behold. Accept your freedom in gratitude and use your freedom to stay free. Follow the hands that set the star in the East so that the holy path will appear ever before you. Listen only for the words of truth. Look only to the heart for what is right and only to God for recognition. Be alert for the signs that you are on course and reach out in welcome to any who would join you. You will be joyous as you go because I am that I am is leading the way.

The springtime of the spirit is glorious for it is the time when the soul sees results, tangible evidence of God in one's personal universe. Solomon in all his glory was not arrayed like one of these. The soul is quickened by the sight and understands why it need take no thought. Who with all his thinking could bring forth such an exquisite canvas? Thou Art.

Springtime fills the soul with gratitude. The eyes and ears feast on its sights and sounds — bees are buzzing with pollen, birds are singing on the backyard fence and folks are laughing in freedom as they emerge from their winter retreat.

Our long winter nap is over and we stretch across the fields of the earth with the words that have woken us. The receiving blanket of life warms us with psalms of divine birth. Springtime wakes us so that we feel alive and on top of the world. Spirit rises directly into our consciousness and we know that we are no longer of the world.

We have escaped the creature whose breathes a life span and knows not the things of God. We become as the meek inheriting the earth, for we have been called and we have heard and we are running to the fields of the Lord. Glory hallelujah is a springtime song of recognition and gratitude. It is the amazing grace that we have found a higher authority, the Lord, King of the universe, to whom we can worship in truth. We have become one with the object of our meditation. "And thou shalt love the Lord, thy God, with all thine heart, with all thy soul and with all thy might." [6]

The days are new in spring for we release on the old. Our heart's desire is revealed at last, freeing us from the weight of false idols that held us down, pinned us back. A buoyant strength fills the body as the courage of our convictions turns from lost hope to faith to surety, from wondering to wonderment. We graduate from mortal weakness to spiritual power for we know that every knee must bow and we have found

Him who drops us to our knees. We have asked for a declaration from the Almighty and He has so declared.

Springtime has given birth to our identity and we no longer need anything from yesterday. It has been purified and left in good order and today the Lord has said, "If ye abide in me, and my words abide in you, ye shall ask what ye will, and it shall be done unto you." [7] Imagine. Ask what ye will and it will be done unto you!

And what is there to ask for from such a Father whose good pleasure it is to give you the kingdom? You have already discovered that nothing of material reality pleases you and that nothing of human sense satisfies your soul. Yet there is one thing left to ask. Lord, reveal thy will. Make known to me your face that I may see your words as they are born from thy mouth that I may dwell in the sacred temple of thy kingdom.

I was blind but spring is here and now I see the everlasting light to which I'm heir. Spring is the season of awe. It restores music to the soul and a constant Companion to sing a love song to the heart. It removes the urgency of fear that ruled the mind and the body, and fills us with love for all living things.

Spring wraps herself around everything with renewed energy and vitality and welcomes the soul's return from hibernation with great and glorious growth.

Every seedling is a saint marching in divine recognition. Every blade of grass that wintered under heavy snow finds its neighbors and lies down in green pasture. A new generation is borne up, exalted at birth and coming as angels to smile upon God's elect and lift them to the mountain top to be anointed of the Lord.

In spring, Life herself is transformed. The lost is found. She has triumphed in her yearning for the infinite and has swaddled her children in the purple robe of omnipresence, omnipotence and omniscience. She has consecrated them in the name of God, I am that I am.

All is well. Spring has brought peace and prosperity to the land as promised. The soul is overjoyed as Spirit offers itself in revelation.

3 *Summer*

School's out. In the summer, the lessons of spirit sink deeply into consciousness. They undo the false ideas of dominion that man's fears have gathered there. A new germination is taking place which will bring forth understanding.

Man has been confounded from "in the beginning." He chose to ignore God's very first instruction which told him that he would die if he ate of the tree of good and evil. He has been dead ever since. He turned down the food that would have sustained him all the days of his life, the trees in the garden he was told he might freely eat, and leaned into his own understanding instead. He has had no peace since, always under the weather with misperception. The moment he swallowed the forbidden fruit, his eyes and ears saw nothing but travail, heard nothing but an inner wailing of desperation.

But the Lord found a good son in Noah and was so well pleased that there was one worthy among men, that he decided to give man another chance at eternity. He gave man new seeds that he might, this time, sow in spirit, rather than flesh, and reap in spirit for there is no reaping in flesh. And many came and planted the new seed and are resting in summer's noonday sun while the germination continues to make them over in their Father's image.

Summer. School is out. Man's teachings have proven to be full of self serving and distorted information, gleaned from the illusions created by his human senses. He must now tune his ears to the frequency of spirit so that the Lord's instruction may be clearly heard, discerned and obeyed. "Then shalt thou walk in thy ways safely, and thy foot shall not stumble. When thou liest down, thou shalt not be afraid; yea, thou shalt lie down, and thy sleep shall be sweet. Be not afraid of sudden fear, neither of desolation of the wicked, when it cometh. For the Lord shall be thy confidence, and shall keep thy foot from being taken." [1]

As you are set free by the paths of righteousness, you manifest summer's daydreams into your experience. The Lord will fulfill your hopes, grant your wishes and honor your aspirations. The relaxing summer of spirit, permanent time off from man's meaningless ways which have left you high and dry, will restore your soul with a passion for life.

One cannot take his own measure any longer for he is blind to the mote in his own eye. "All the ways of a man are clean in his own eyes; but the Lord weighest the spirits." [2]

And what of your spirit? Is it known unto you? Have you come by its loving touch and been blessed by its grace and opened to its truths? Have you learned that you are God's child all the days of your life, this one and those to come? Summer is the season to rest in sure knowledge of the eternal. No longer need you swim upstream where man's confusion has set its compass. Go with the flow to the land of summer's sweet milk and honey. Take the time so that life's meaning can catch up with you.

Do not be a scholar who takes satisfaction in what he knows for what he knows gives him pride but not joy. All too soon the season will change and he will have only yesterday's word to live by while the others will reap the great harvest of revelation. The Lord will speak to those with ears to hear. Listen and you will hear.

Your days are laid out for you in divine order. Every one of them has been set to serve a purpose and as you serve it, your blessings will be released to your name. You will hardly believe what a true harvest looks like and feels like but it will be familiar nonetheless. You are returned to the house of the Lord from whence you came.

Your world is a private affair with God. Your life is shared in a living, breathing consciousness of your God and your brothers. "Hear oh Israel, the Lord our God. The Lord is one." [3]

Summer's consciousness has been long awaited. After the active winter of discontent and the bustling spring of rebirth, the lazy, hazy days of summer bring meditative quiet. Peace be still. Summer quietly seeps into the protected husk of the ears of corn and makes golden sweet the little brother and sister kernels as they snuggle together in their cozy nest. All is grace.

In summer you realize that you're no longer up against any problems for the grace has smoothed their edges and laid bare the illusions that created them. You rise up to the simple joy of understanding, jump rope in the newly found freedom of spirit, swing in the hammock of gratitude.

Summer spells out recognition that there is a Sabbath after all. It raises consciousness to a world where there are more people for you than against you. It takes one out on a Sunday drive of contentment and liberates the soul. Hush now, don't you cry. The Lord's in His heaven and all's right with the world.

With all the free time that summer offers including the sweet fulfillment of restored faith, one must still stay the high watch. Too much time in the sun without proper protection burns the skin. One must take one's freedom joyously but seriously. Great truths may be taken for granted only when all the world recognizes them and lives by their divine principles. Until then, one must enjoy freedom yet be mindful of its future. Keep it out of the way of those who would tempt you to share it. Their time will come but first they must do the work of it. Something for nothing is not a divine exchange. It will lose in value and before you know it, two hot headed gamblers will be fighting for the last shred of clothing worn by a holy man.

You who read the words of summer's soul are beloved of the Lord "For they are life unto those that find them, and health to all their flesh." [4] It is in the warmth of forgiveness that the soul ripens. As the teaching of the school year spends the summer reworking itself into learning, understanding and knowing, forgiveness emerges as the valedictorian of virtues. It speaks out in humility and grace. The earth melts at its' voice and the temple is rebuilt on pillars of prayer and praise. "To everything there is a season, and a time to every purpose under the heaven." [5]

At last we fulfill our mission. We find God and we hear His commandment, "That ye love one another."[6]

Summer is sweet surrender. The soul opens its eyes to the great rays of spirit's revelation which lights up everything in blazing perfection.

Man graduates from the school of mortal beliefs and is no longer bound by the limits of faulty perceptions. He has come to understand that his physical eyes deceive him. They tell him that the world is flat, and that people die. Now he knows better. He has acquired spiritual tools of perception and they do not deceive him. His capacity to discern the truth not only increases at graduation but will ever increase for that is its substance, its very quality. It is an omnipresent I am unfolding as the daily bread of consciousness. No sooner does spiritual vision emerge than it doubles in size, triples in scope and then again and again until all it can see is eternity and infinity. It is a panoramic view of forever.

Once one graduates man's school and steps into the spiritual world, he is at a point of no return. An illusion once revealed can never be again mistaken. This does not mean it's time to go back to sleep for the capacity to discern the truth is ever increasing. Yesterday's man and yesterday's manna was sufficient only for yesterday. Each day is the time for us to once more recognize and serve our purpose; it is what the day is for and why it is given into our keeping. To each new day we must say yes, each and every day.

Many truths remain to be learned for by the time we come by the tools to discern them we have much to undo. We must purge erroneous conclusions by which we have been living and abandon the negative thoughts that have been directing our activities. We must make room for the lost years of the locust to return.

Most people don't know that they are spiritually asleep

so that when one awakes he finds himself alone. He is no longer in the classroom listening and reciting among thirty five others but reading his summer book of spirit by himself.

It is a grand discovery to be alone. One can finally hear one's own heart beating and own thoughts and feelings in peace. Without the earthly teacher ready to pronounce right! wrong! to our every answer and without the earthly parent ready to censor every thought and feeling that falls outside his own beliefs, one can enter in and have a look at God's ways.

Beyond human reasoning which offers man only its own version of truth, are the glorious revelations which will turn you upside down and inside out with understanding. You do not have to die to get to God's heaven. That is man's heaven. God's heaven is your consciousness which you can expand right now. You have the time, for it is summer soulstice. You have the space for you are alone. And you have the information for "The voice of the Lord is upon the waters: The God of glory thundereth: ..." [7]

Take hold of yourself and enter the kingdom of heaven now. Let the old world go and use your key to open the God door, for everything your heart hopes for is fulfilled behind it. The Lord has all His promises in divine order ready to unfold unto you as you recognize that they are yours, held for you, until you ask. Yes, you must ask. You are a graduate student of spirit and you have learned that God is unable to deliver truth to the unprepared thought lest it fall on deaf ears. Have you not tried to impart your wisdom to another who would have none of it?

Welcome to your successful matriculation in the things of spirit. You may enter at will and at the mere drop of an inspiration. Nothing can hold you back for nothing can prevail against the will of God. You may be seen of the Father for it is every parent's wish to behold the child. All your schooling has been to bring you to this time and place.

This is a holy day. This is a sacred moment. You are no longer summer daydreaming but standing on the holy ground of recognition. The Lord your God has called you to Him and you are hearing. The wild stirring that you feel inside is the changing of the guard. New vibrations are on the march and they will keep you from harm's way. You are free at last, free from the bondage of an old consciousness. You are consecrated in the spirit and unto you is revealed the purpose of your birth.

Summer has fulfilled itself. It prepared you to become a member of the remnant that the Lord held out that you might rise to the mighty works before you. Seek only to find that which is past finding out and, "According to your faith, be it unto you." [8]

4 Fall

Leave summer with a final nod at the things of olde but be ye not wistful, for the true desires of your heart are about to unfold and they will be unto you forevermore, forever more. It is in the fall that nature fulfills herself for it is the time of harvest. It is the moment when the sowing and the reaping meet in manifestation. It is the moment of truth.

Those who have sowed to spirit will fall on their knees in gratitude as they recognize and receive the bounty of God's grace. It will fill the granary once and for all and they need no longer take thought. Their unfolded consciousness realizes that there is a perpetual harvest, an endless supply of grace.

Those who hear the word of the Lord which commands them not to eat of the tree of good and evil are no longer lost in the mortal world of duality. They will bear a son who offers the first fruits to the Lord and who does not, therefore, try to hide his shame by taking up the life of his brother. God's favor is unlimited. It shines down on all who look to Him and there is enough to light every soul. If thine eye be single, one could not handle all the riches stored in his name.

God's infinite supply exists at the very moment when man turns away from the finite fields of world mind. This finite amount leaves him instantly hungry and he inevitably spends life trying to increase it. Impossible. World mind cannot be increased, only decreased. Only that which has substance can grow. Illusions must of their nature come to nothing.

The Lord himself is the harvest. Nothing more is to be manifest. The new heaven and the new earth are reality. Watch lava from an active volcano flow into the water and cool into brand new land. It is a great sight to behold. If man would search out his bones and marrow for signs of God, he would find the source of increase which he was seeking and flesh himself out in its spirit.

Man's attraction to worldly wealth causes him to worship every man named Rich for inspiration. The world, however, is full of Rich men but they are merely Cain in disguise and the moment you seek their company, they will sweep down and make of you a beggar or a dead man. Worldly wealth will promise much and then watch you like a hawk less you decrease one jot of its' lion's share. It will throw you down and slay you with greed as you bend down to look for any meat on the bones which it has thrown you. The more you try to climb man's ladder of success, the more you will waste yet another precious moment, another holy day. Even if you get to dip your hand into a pot of gold, all you will see when you go to count is a lot of ashes and a load of rust and corruption.

The money trail is an object lesson in futility and self destruction. Leave it and don't look back. Count your blessings that you are able to get on with it. If you look back you will only see the last of man as he sinks in the quicksand that swallows the worshippers of worldly wealth.

The harvest is not money. It is the wondrous realization of truth. It is the essence of fulfillment for those who look to God as their supply. God's abundance is dependable for he is always present and pays not in diminished returns but with great dividend.

When a man becomes spiritually seasoned, he recognizes that money is the root of all evil because it is just the beginning, the root, of seeking the treasures of the material world while becoming blind to their source. Nothing of the world's harvest touches one's soul or the bottom of his heart. It delights his senses, makes him look good to his neighbors and causes temporary satisfaction of his personal will. It also leaves him on empty, for his soul still has an innate need to be touched and his heart will always pine for its own. All too soon after he has counted his money and exclaimed, "Oh, what a good boy am I" he will cry "Oh woe is me!"

It is time to reap at the great harvest once and for all time. Leave the world of overworked, infertile soil. Come to the final harvest, the reaping of an understanding that will carry you to the heights of the deep and to the breadth of the narrow road. God's harvest will yield the holy of holies, lifting your soul to soar with the angels, no longer subject to the crop failure of man's sowing to the flesh.

Fall honors the tenderness and the labor of love with which man has planted the seeds of his spirit, protecting them from devouring birds, shallow earth, scorching sun and choking weeds. When the bread appears, it is enough to feed the multitudes. God is omnipotent. Given just a little to go on, just a seed no bigger than a grain of mustard seed, He will add to your harvest more than you have planted.

Fall is the reaping of the fruit that does not fall far from the tree which God placed in the Garden for food. As man has wrestled with the long arms of temptation which have tried to envelop him in every word and deed, he has learned that all else fails but truth. At last he can put down his mind's hoe and let truth's reaper declare the way he should go. It leads him straight to the bottom of his heart where the harvest has been waiting for a signal before bursting out in infinite manifestation. "And ye shall eat in plenty; and be satisfied; and praise the name of the Lord your God, that hath dealt wondrously with you; and my people shall never be ashamed." [1]

Fall is, in reality, you, gloriously clothed in the autumn colors of spirit. You have harvested the beloved into your soul and your flesh manifests the golden glow of revelation. You have come to the throne of your own spiritual coronation and have earned dominion over the earth and the fullness thereof. Your heavenly father has bestowed his blessing upon your reign. Your sovereignty is supreme, subject only to the laws of truth.

You are now gloriously arrayed like the lilies of the field and your crown jewels will reflect the Lord's intense light that it might lead people to recognize their sanctity. You stand on the holy ground of the promised land, delivered from the bondage of slavery in which your faithlessness imprisoned you. You have crossed the Red Sea of disbelief and returned to the Garden with wisdom and understanding. You shall lead a nation to recognize thy kingdom come, on Earth, as it is in heaven. You are become a true shepherd of the Lord's will.

You have walked through the valley of the shadow of death and recognized it as a shadow - a mere fear that had no substance, no depth, no reality. Only life is truth. Only truth is life.

You are beloved of the Lord. He has laid out the crooked road into a straight and narrow path and you have followed it all the way home. Your harvest is a golden mountain of divine recognition, so infinite that you can no longer count your blessings but find yourself fallen to your knees in praise and gratitude. "How amiable are thy tabernacles, O Lord of hosts!" [2]

The Lord has placed his blessing upon you. It is your daily bread, enough to fill you to overflowing. The rock from which the manna flows into daily harvest will sustain you today and tomorrow. It will refill with enough supply for an everlasting journey. The Lord's word does not return to him void. Everyone who ever sent you blessings or said God Bless You was adding to your supply.

When you lay down to sleep under God's great comforter, the bread you have eaten today will feed your soul. Unto this day is the revelation that there is not one harvest but harvest after harvest. There is one autumn after another and you reap again and again until the lost years of the locust are returned and you become one with the earth and abide forever in her keeping. Your vision will soar and give you a clear view of life's spiritual food supply from now until forever.

The harvest sinks deep into the crucible of your understanding and reveals the unfolding of man as the changing of the seasons. In the winter, he is cold, beaten back by ice, rain, sleet and snow. He is humbled by his helplessness. In spring, he finds his faith, for the Lord sends signs, glorious signs of renewal and light. Summer brings him rest. He is warm, well fed, enjoying the Sabbath of his days. And from his sweet slumber, he arises to the great Fall harvest that has made him over in the image of his maker.

The seasons of the earth evolve man from an unconscious creature to a conscious one, from one who lives only as one with the world to one who lives only as one with his Creator. He is healed of all that has ailed him. That which ailed him, his own winter of disbelief, has passed and his flesh will not kill him with fear or old age. See if this isn't so. Wake to your God and see if he gave life but to take it away.

To everything to which there was a season your season has arrived. Your purpose is manifest. The time for you to bow your knees has come upon you. Behold, the Lord has chosen this season to be revealed unto you. Let him not find that you are still seeking a final frontier.

Your days on earth are numbered but in the spirit they are not. Where, therefore, will you cast your net and under whose wings will you seek your tailwind? You do not have to make up your mind but merely to listen. The answer will become evident. "In the way of righteousness is life; and in the pathway thereof there is no death."[3]

It is time to expand your horizon to include the recognition that God is all there is. In the spirit of matter and in the matter of spirit, you may finally stop wanting or needing more than the day already holds in store. The grains of truth in the sands of time are but a drop in the bucket of the blessings which will be bestowed on you who recognize, "This is the day the Lord has made; we will rejoice and be glad in it." [4]

REFERENCES

Page 64 1 Genesis 1:2

Page 64 2 II Corinthians 12:9

Page 65 3 I Samuel 3:9

Page 66 4 Isaiah 30:21

Page 68 5 Leviticus 20:7-8

Page 69 6 Isaiah 45:3

Page 74 1 Psalm 30:5

Page 74 2 Proverbs 1:33

Page 74 3 Isaiah 40:5

Page 75 4 Genesis 1:31

Page 75 5 Psalm 30:11-12

Page 78 6 Deuteronomy 6:5

Page 79 7 John 15:7

Page 81 1 Proverbs 3:23-26

Page 81 2 Proverbs 16:2

Page 82 3 Deuteronomy 6:4

Page 83 4 Proverbs 4:22

Page 83 5 Ecclesiastes 3:1

Page 83 6 John 15:12

Page 85 7 Psalms 29:3

Page 86 8 Matthew 9:29

Page 89 1 Joel 2:26

Page 90 2 Psalms 84:1

Page 91 3 Proverbs 12:28

Page 92 4 Psalms 118:24

"And the Lord answered me and said, Write the vision, and make it plain upon tables, that he may run that readeth it.

"For the vision is yet for an appointed time, but at the end it shall speak, and not lie: though it tarry, wait for it; because it will surely come ..."

Habakkuk 2:2-3

THE
SACRED LIFE

BOOK IV

TABLE OF CONTENTS

THE EYE OPENING

The call from Spirit is the only temptation that weighs positive on the balance beam of life and yet the only one we resist. Perhaps because it whispers softly rather than clanging loudly do we miss its beautiful invitation to a sacred life. We are so used to having our senses bombarded by the salesmen of material reality that the gems of timeless value remain discreetly beyond our vision.

It is always a good time to close the shop of mortal thought for a moment and take inventory of our souls. The spiritual life has a tendency to get dusty because we relegate it to the back shelf or to the upper one that is hard to reach. Out of sight, out of mind, it sits patiently with inestimable worth waiting to be come upon by anyone who perchance stops before it.

You are, indeed, very blessed. Having slowed down to have a look around, you are the one who has discovered the prize.

Upon you, holy one of God, will be bestowed the pearl of great price ...

1 *Spiritual Reality*

Reality has a way of responding to a variety of definitions. In the hands of a physicist, it takes shape and form using the language of time and space whereas in the life of a baby it means warm milk and a rocking cradle.

Spiritual reality similarly can mean different things to different people. Those who find comfort in religion are unlike those who profess atheism and those who live in the Taoism of the east do not see eye to eye with the Judeo Christian expression of the west.

Yet, for all the differences or similarities of reality and their definitions, the truth of the matter is that all of life is a holy manifestation of God, nothing else. Man simply chooses to interpret it according to his current experience, training or tradition. If he finds satisfaction in his beliefs, he will state his case, rest his cause and file his conclusions under the appropriate name, alternatively titled science, philosophy or religion.

For some, the fortunate ones, the flow of information stops short of the ring of truth. Left unsure in a world whose answers don't reach as far as his questions, he is guided by an inner prompting to hold for a different verdict than the jury has submitted. Having had the fortitude to go it alone, he stands recognized as a seeker, a member of the remnant whom God has chosen for himself. As he stays the course, he will behold the pearl of great price.

The territory of the fourth dimension is populated by the consciousness that recognizes the truth couched between the lines of man's mortal agenda. He who walks in grace abandons the fear that attacks the human senses in the third dimension, and moves to a higher vibration. It is the courage of faith, not the courage of fear, in which his mystical feet take the journey. He professes nothing, only reaches out in regal bearing to offer you the company of angels as you both head for home.

God speaks in a language that only those who have ears to hear can understand. Anyone may develop the ears to hear once he has removed them from the tutelage of world mind, mortal thought or material reality. Those ears only hear popular opinion and screeching headlines. If it were not for the high volume of empty promises and misleading directions, they would not hear anything at all. They are as good soldiers waiting for the sound of fury, signifying nothing.

The Lord does not live in man's noisy world. He takes no notice of man's proclamations or his laws.

Neither does he hear man's sense of quiet which is merely the absence of his noise. That which man calls quiet can be heard in any cemetery. Mark thee well. Quiet is not the sound of the Lord.

Ears that truly hear turn away from man's quiet and lean toward the deeper frequency, Silence. This is the holy channel for it is on this wavelength that the Lord broadcasts. One must come to this listening with great reverence, for Silence is not the same thing as quiet. Silence is the presence of God. It skips a thousand words and whispers the message directly to the inner ear. It lifts the words of death off men's tombstones and blasts them through the trumpet of everlasting life.

2 *Truth Seeking*

The chosen of God do not recognize themselves at first. It does not please them that they are discontent in the face of plenty. They do not understand why they feel differently than their more content brothers and sisters nor do they perceive it as a positive experience. Only after prolonged unhappiness do they come to realize that there is more to life than meets the eye and they hunger to find out what it is. The moment they begin to search out new direction, spiritual sensitivities emerge on cue.

So does the seeker begin to recognize himself and set his sights on a more fulfilling experience. He will not have long to wait. The spiritual life is a responsive life. No sooner does one become aware of its possibilities than it begins to send signals that it has been recognized. This may be proven to any one at any time as long as the seeker is of a sincere heart and earnest intention. The Lord is too pure to perceive iniquity and will not, cannot, materialize to human sense.

The early signs of spiritual unfoldment are the same at every stage of the journey. Whether one is setting down his first footprint or has had a lamp unto his feet for thousands of miles, it is always a loud Silence that presses into the surroundings. Things appear to the physical eyes and ears as before but one gets the distinct impression that he possesses these tools of perception rather than being one with them. This distinction, subtle but definite, gives man a sense of an intervening agency so that he does not perceive that he is one with what he sees or hears but one with a Self that is doing the seeing or hearing. The newcomer can find this experience intensely startling and unsettling but the spiritual old timer welcomes it greatly. He knows another piece of fruit has ripened on the tree of life and is about to fertilize the holy ground beneath him.

Although life bustles us about in an endless display of give and take, we actually live and make choices according to the subtle impressions that impinge on our flesh from moment to moment. Mortal man, hearing quiet, perceives it as an empty space and immediately sets himself to fill it. He thinks, acts, talks, plans, measures, moves, anything to keep himself feeling alive lest the void swallow him in death before he has lived his life, before he has risen in glory. His entire viewpoint places him as the main character on the stage of life and his entire thrust is to produce and direct the play with a happy ending and an Oscar for his performance.

Man of spirit is unlike the man of the world. When the curtain comes up on a spiritual being, he drops to his knees as the sound of Silence pierces his formerly deaf ears and fills the empty space with God. "Speak Lord, for thy servant heareth."[1] He feels his very flesh becoming heir to spirit and his very life becoming immortal. He can hear the applause of saints and angels, whose invisible hands are clapping at his arrival into heaven. He has won the ready, set, go of man's race to conquer death. Oscar has become a mere piece of metal, another clanging symbol.

Man of spirit, how holy you are. Do you know how rare it is to recognize the impress of the sacred amidst the thousand tentacles of mortal life competing to wrap you in their illustrious illusions. Welcome to the ark of the holy of holies. You have survived the flood. Two by two, you and God, under the bow he has set in the clouds as a token of the covenant between you, go forth in perpetuity for the water shall no more become a flood unto you or yours.

Blessed are you for you have heard the Silence and the Silence is the shell which the pearl of great price calls home.

3 *Great Is Your Reward*

Spiritual consciousness requires a thorough reworking of mortality's system of reward. Man is ever poised to perceive his identity in the mirror of external feedback. A constant supply of recognition is required on an ongoing basis.

He feeds off each compliment and locks it into his flesh, storing up the extras for the lean times of insecurity. Every pat on the back insures the even flow of supply to his intravenous life line, having to prove again and again to his mortal life that he is alive. An invitation to anywhere by anyone catapults his self esteem off the charts.

Man has cornered himself in the bullring of human experience and gambled on his very life. His reality rises and falls on the fickle and arbitrary testimony of man who would as soon charge at him and gore him to death for entertainment than point him toward safety's gate. Yet one must not waste pity on one who would make himself into a life sized puppet and offer the strings to the highest bidder. Time is better served in contemplation of a worthier fate.

The rewards that man is really after are right under foot. If he would but look, he could see that the ripe fruit has indeed fallen on holy ground.

Come now to the reward that spirit would have you receive. At the moment you turn from the mortal who simply cannot collect enough trophies, the gifts of spirit will start their infinite flow into your experience. Open out your arms, they will not be wide enough to carry your treasures. Nothing of your current belief can conceive beyond the limit of the container which you have etched and locked in place in your mind. Your mortal experience has convinced you that there is a price for everything, that nothing is free, nothing easy. In mortal experience, that is true. In spirit, however, supply is greater than any demand, no matter how great it is or how impossible it seems.

If you bring consciousness to God's altar, you will begin to learn what reward truly is, how great it really feels, how deep it truly goes, how high its ultimately reaches. And this is just the beginning, just today's manna ... Your eyes could never see all the reward He has for you, for your eyes only, for mortal eyes can only see as far as the horizon.

God is the gift giver, the very gift. Expand your vision right now so that the flow of reward can start streaming toward the open door of your heart. It will flow and flow, forever and ever, from a bottomless well. You have not been dreaming. All that you imagined for yourself is ready to materialize from the infinite invisible into the shape and form that will fill the size of the cup that you lift.

The reward you get from the Lord's eyes will render any compliment, any gift, any recognition from the world as a mere pittance, one lump of coal that will ignite the fire for one second of a cold winter. You have no idea, truly, no idea of your reward for it is not a thought, but a reality, in the dispensing hands of spirit.

You may rest. You may stop wishing and hoping and pleading and doubting and crying. Look up. You have merely to move out of the neighborhood of man whose baker brings a daily bread of fear and doubt, and relocate yourself in the company of spirit.

God is God. You have yet to enjoy all that He is, all that He wills for you. Your mind has used thought to appropriate Him and your thought changes from moment to moment. Your belief becomes doubt in one moment and then returns to belief at the Sunday meetin'. Back and forth, swayed between the high and mighty and the Almighty.

Oh, man, come ye to the well. Join the chorus of angels who have lowered the bucket and raised up a new vision, a kingdom where the king brings You the gifts. Walk down the aisle of this King, and earth will swallow up the man king and heaven will appear. For your eyes only, the powerful yes of spirit will remove yesterday's meager showing and part the great iron gates of heaven's treasury and invite you in. Seek ye first the kingdom of heaven, see ye first the king, and all else will follow, more reward than you eyes can conceive for you are worth more than you claim. Soon ye will know...

4 *Time Is Of the Essence*

Mortal reality is constantly piling up things to do. Any sense of time for ourselves is pushed to the weekend, the vacation, the sick bed, the retirement. Somewhere out there is a lifetime lounge chair with nothing left to do but nothing.

As much as life urges us toward self expression or requires us to fill the coffers, we act with an unconscious conclusion that there is "not enough time." Mortal life crowds itself into our space with demands that accept no excuses and no tardiness. It expresses them with an air of such urgency that we pressurize behind its surgeon's mask and conduct ourselves under the razor's edge of emergency room readiness.

Peace. "Be still and know that I am God."[1] The time of your life is not yet to come, it is merely a pearl waiting for a diver. As you seek ye first the kingdom of heaven, time will appear from nowhere for it was not stored in the future where you placed it. It is stored in the present consciousness, saved only for recognition.

As you look to spirit first and last, the alpha and the omega, the load on your shoulders is carried out by a greater force than you can bring to bear from mental or physical gymnastics. No matter how visionary the physicist, no matter how high the mathematician, they cannot capture and tame the absolute, nor square infinity into their formulae. The universe is an invitation to life but, "The earth is the Lord's, and the fullness thereof; the world, and they that dwell therein."[2] Man can merely bring himself to the limit of his mind, where he will forever "run out of time." Let him rather cross over into divine time and have a look around.

As man beholds his busy, mortal self from the witness stand of infinite consciousness, he will perceive his busyness as a cover up, disguising his yearning for the infinite behind his fear of the intimate. God is ever close, so near that man will overfill every moment rather than grant any homage to a higher power. He is still unfinished with the belief in worldly recognition and continues to arch his back that he may hug the glory to himself.

One moment of surrender to the truth of his being will ignite the divine breath into his physical lungs. He will discover that time is a gift from the Lord, and not an illusion that man has placed in the hands of a clock or in the far reaches of his imagination for use at a later date. "... but the time is coming when I will no longer speak to you in figurative language, but I will tell you plainly about the Father." [3]

Rest in peace this moment, this day, in every thing you do, that you may thereby eliminate the need to seek a grave so that you can catch up. Death is not a final resting place. It is an idea that the collective of world mind created to deal with the everlasting postponement of the moment of truth.

You are the beloved child of God. Permit yourself but one moment, this moment, to feel this truth and you will learn of life everlasting where time is of the essence of God and therefore it will never run out, never abandon you, never forsake you.

You may stand at ease. Divine consciousness will instantly and in any instance dispel the erroneous conclusion that there is a race going on. It will deliver you successfully to live in the full grace of each moment as you stand in the recognition that there is a higher power, and that it rests in you.

5 *Expanding the Borders*

Consciousness is a very present state of affairs. It is the unfolding and ongoing communication between flesh and spirit.

As one begins to discern that his human senses fail him time and again, he becomes confused. Told by mortal reality that what he sees in black and white is real and that what is real is called the truth, he cannot understand why things turn out poorly.

He listens to what the law says, but though his ears hear it, the outcome does not reflect the justice of which it speaks. Though he puts in a good day's effort, others lay claim to some of the fruit he has garnered and call it their own. Even his own friends claim, often as not, that an eye for an eye is an equal trade off.

Slowly but surely, sinking under the weight of mortal thought and his own unhappiness, man faces his first important choice. He can join his brothers and get a fair share of the take, including membership in their club and all its tokens, or stand apart and take them on. Either way, he locks himself in battle and his rewards will be long in their coming, short on their satisfaction.

When man takes the world on its word, he is forced to choose up sides because that is what he has learned. He is born to a world of duality that sets up the conditions from the start, right verses wrong, might verses right, good verses evil. He is pulled by opposing arguments while the platitudes tell him to keep an open mind. Regardless of how he chooses, the other side waits with its judgment, forcing him into a perpetual volley of second guessing. He is the ball, ping ponging between fierce opponents and unable to perceive an escape route.

The escape route does exist, however. It is merely outside of the human sense. One must leave the game in order to be neither the pawn nor the player. He must perceive a different vision altogether. Behind the obvious, and above the boundary of world thought, is the rule of grace. It is born of spiritual sense and requires only that one keep his eye focused on God, first, foremost, only and always. God is the answer, the outcome, the revelator of all that is. Only in beholding God, may man do away with the sad duel of duality, where the winner is declared as the one who subjugates his brother.

Superiority is the biggest coward of all and yet man seeks its mantle as the ultimate prize. Thank God that there are some who come to us in deliverance and utter the words, "He that hath clean hands, and a pure heart; who hath not lifted up his soul unto vanity, nor sworn deceitfully ... shall receive the blessing from the Lord, and righteousness from the God of his salvation."[1]

As citizens of spirit, we must pledge ourselves only to truth for therein is the only path that is wide enough to accommodate the footprints of all men. It is the only path that marks the holy ground of peace and leads us home.

The borders of your tent may be enlarged at any time and, indeed, every time you expand them the more you will see manifestations of spirit in your life. Just as a sponge has a greater capacity to hold water than appears by its dimensions, and a balloon can take in more air than the eye would guess, one who efforts on behalf of spirit will increase the capacity to perceive God and to receive His blessings.

The map is not the territory. The map is man's estimation of the territory. It misses by the extent of the soul which cannot be measured.

6 *The Works of Spirit*

The spiritual life is a different experience of life than that which precedes it. It attracts everyone now and then, always at a moment of crises or futility, but rarely does a human stay the course. Once the extreme position that allows him to call to Spirit retracts, man retreats to the familiar life of yesteryear and goes about business as usual. Only when he once more has stuffed his doubts and fears under the rug of mortality and is out of room, does he come around again to renew his courtship of God. And so forth.

Although man knows that the Lord gets him out of trouble when he earnestly makes an appeal, he rarely chooses to keep company on a permanent basis. This is beyond the comprehension of those who make God the center of their lives, who use their time on earth to carry out His will.

The spiritual life, for those who choose it, unfolds in a perpetual sense of grandeur and wonder. Surrendered to a deeper awareness that God perfects everything that concerns them, any worries that arise are quickly passed through the strainer of fear without time to wad into serious matter. Without bits and pieces of negativity incessantly darkening everything they touch, the natural vibration of spirit roams freely throughout their consciousness, filling it with an ongoing sense of recognition, joy and gratitude. They that experience this fourth dimensional consciousness learn that the works of it insure the outcome every time and they therefore become its faithful adherents. The works are simple, for divine principles are constantly revealing the choices and spirit always decides for spirit.

The works of spirit are beyond no man for they accompany his physical birth and come into his knowing at prescribed times. In every moment that you perceive a problem and behave in the highest, even in the face of the dimmest, you have given the Lord his opportunity to intervene on your behalf. When you tell the truth, although a lie would be easier, when you forgive a betrayer though you'd prefer revenge, when you love one another rather than steal the prize, you enter the remarkable territory of holy ground.

Rising to spirit's heights, one checks the first appearance of fruit to make sure it is ripe. Often things look good at the beginning and before we have given it any spiritual consideration, we heave it off the tree and swallow it whole. The bitter taste tells us we have overreacted and that we have not only failed to satisfy our hunger, we have increased it. Even when we can discern the true fruit from the good seed, we must still not eat for we must offer the first fruits to God.

The ability and willingness to hold our human hunger in check for just one spiritual moment becomes the strength and confidence we need to feed ourselves and our loved ones ever after. There is plenty left over for the armies but there are no armies, for there is nothing to fight for. The spiritual food that follows the human fast is a feast that never ends. Supply and demand is a mortal concept and does not exist in the holy land because the Lord does not starve his children. Man does that.

While spiritual fruit is ripening on the tree of life, a man of spirit listens with his inner ear to the ways he should go. There is always a fresh load of manna. The Lord's will is precise, clear and comes with directions that are unmistakable. Man only gets lost when he fails to ask for them or neglects to heed them. Over and over must he check in, for his mind and his understanding lead him away from his destination, "For my thoughts are not your thoughts, neither are your ways my ways..."[1] These will be given unto you who ask.

Trust that the works of spirit are not new words nor words that take thought. They will not confound you. They are simply carried out in the name of, in the light of, in the spirit of the Lord, thy God.

In every instance take the high road. Don't do anything which will create the need to apologize, to defend yourself, to make you wish you had had more patience, exercised more kindness, shown more mercy, been more open minded, kept the faith, showed your love. Give the best of your best even when no one is there to notice or to take account or to give just reward. Claim no special privilege; do not blame the guilty or defend the innocent. Speak the truth in every moment and suffer any consequence while they are inconsequential.

When the Lord decides that your moment has come, bow down, sweet spirit. You will not believe the glory that will be heaped on your head. It will be but a tiny token of the glory you have shown to God. You will need every moment forthcoming to receive the rest, every moment of eternity, for there is no limit to what is coming your way ...

7 *Infinite Goodness*

In the realm of spirit everything is spirit. Spirit is the parent of everything that comes forth in the universe. The life of man is eternal for it is conceived and birthed from the life of spirit which is everlasting. Like begets like.

When man comes into the flesh, he forgets his true nature. Although he professes to believe in goodness, he is ever in doubt and ends up forever protecting himself from the fear that it creates. As he judges others, the judgments return to him multiplied and he is unable to perceive how he has generated them himself. He feels ever at risk. As he steals from others to protect himself he believes that robbers are ever at his door. He lies and believes that all men are deceivers. The idea of turning the other cheek to dismantle the adversary is beyond his conception, for pride and vanity have blocked his understanding. He simply becomes increasingly afraid.

When man is scared he makes five thousand laws and foregoes the five thousand blessings that are at hand. The powerful rod of Moses turns to a serpent in his own hand at every turn. As man continues to err in his human condition, spirit continues to forgive, for it has not judged. It is man himself who flounders, fails and falls, for he has no thing to lift him up. As he has no idea or no desire to turn to the omnipotence of God, he repeats the same futile process and enacts the same unhappy endings all the days of his life. War within, war without.

Any moment that a man is willing to swallow his pride long enough to cry out his defeat in earnest, life will extend a helping hand. It is the nature of goodness to recognize where and to whom it shall come bearing gifts. Good things rarely happen to man who believeth only in himself for man is only nostril until the Lord gives him breath. Man will create the appearance of good but without God to maintain and sustain it, nothing good can survive its illusionary substance.

Once man is truly on his knees, not needing "just one more time" but finally and forever in recognition that there is no life without God, he will learn the nature of goodness and grace. He will soar with the angels, looking at his past in amazement of his former belief that he could go it alone.

Lord, take my best. Let me learn how to put into practice my love for you. Teach me faith and patience that I may expand my consciousness and live ever after in the arms of your infinite goodness.

8 *The Ladder of Illusion*

Man is very pleased with himself. He has learned to fool most of the people most of the time. Leaving the house, his last look in the mirror assures him that he can handle the challenges of his day and return home before anyone discovers that he is a fraud. Although he would like to actually feel the way he pretends to feel, he regards life as a drama and believes the best actor winds up with the best part. He is holding out for his.

If he successfully fools himself, man lifts his chin, squares his shoulders and decorates himself with self respect.

When he fails to achieve status in his own eyes, unable to score the appropriate script, he shrugs as if he didn't care, claiming that the rules aren't fair, that the part isn't right.

Whether man perceives himself on the highest rung of the ladder or the lowest, he has no conception that the ladder itself is all in his own mind.

When a wake up call comes, man is very blessed for he no longer has to balance on the high beam with tired legs or start another futile climb only to wait forever for something that is not forthcoming. He recognizes, instead, that he is a man of spirit and it is the spirit of man that doeth the works.

As he lets the Lord lift his burdens, the morning mirror sends him forth in utter confidence. When the voice of man tempts him to fall back under the blanket of doubt and fear, he need merely stop and listen, for such a voice will be drowned out by a louder One which will proclaim "... whither thou goest-I will go ..."[1] and there shall I be evermore.

It is in the best interest of man that he use every opportunity to remove the image of every ladder that he has falsely constructed and cemented in his mind. As he begins to burn the rungs of misperception on the fires of surrender, he will see in the mirror that he is being made over in the image of his maker. As he employs the workings of the mind in service to spirit, his downfall from the ladder of illusion will prop him up simply and gracefully on the holy ground beneath him.

9 *What News Is This?*

What is the news? Everyone wants news. The senses of man are primed to be stirred, ever hungry for the next stimulation so that he may know what to think, what move to make. Shall he get yesterday's news with which to gossip, sad news with which to complain or bad news over which to become fearful. There's a chance he might even get good news but although he lives for it, good news is always followed by bad or comes attached to a hook, better not get caught. Pray for it but hush, don't tell a soul, then no one will know that underneath there is another, the hopeful one, the one who aches to be set free of any news at all since truly, for him it is never good.

Oh, man, look at those senses and give them a rest. They are taking you to misery's door and the grave that lies behind it. You are knocking yourself out, leaving nothing one way or the other. Your senses are making of you a mere knee jerk, the mere shell of a man. Dear one, dare yourself to step forward into the light, out of range of every shot in the dark which leaves you a drowning victim of disillusionment. Step out of the tidal wave. It holds you captive at the high water mark and uses you up treading for survival.

There is news, good news, all good, only good, permanent and everlasting. It is ready for the eyes and ears of your soul, given you automatically the moment you rest your senses and let your spirit come into view and hearing range. The high water matter will subside. You may catch your breath, your new breath, one which will relax and float you home.

Spirit is another name for good news. You may let your secret escape for there will be no more crushed hope. When a thing is real, there is no power greater than it to crush it. There is no empty space to reduce its size. The substance is the same throughout. Spirit is the only solid gold, backed by full faith and is a credit to the eyes that have closed to the appearance of things and opened to the truth that holy is all there is, holy is all that does.

10 *Pray Aright*

Invisible does not mean that a thing cannot be seen. It means it cannot be seen by you. If it could not be seen by any, there would not be a word to describe its degree of visibility.

What is it that you would like to bring into your own vision? If you answer in worldly terms, you may or, most probably may not, see anything at all. The material world operates on principles of may the better man win, with no thought that the better man may be a deceiver. You will be at the mercy of deception as well as greed and manipulation. Even if you manage to realize your dream, the one in line after you will be waiting to seize it or, failing that, sabotage it so that if he can't have it, neither can you. Failing even that, he will tax it, insist you insure it, guilt trip you into sharing it, or make you doubt its value. He will not leave you any peace. The "better man" is an idea whose time has run out. Men are equal in the eyes of the Lord.

The material world operates on another false principle as well, one that will make your holdings hard to come by and even harder to keep. That principle is called scarcity. Scare city. Man believes that there are more people waiting a thing than there are things to go around. The entire economic system of mortal thought is based on demand. No one knows a mortal man better than another mortal man for they are both convinced that a thing of value is a joy forever. What they don't know is what a thing of value is. To them it appears as something of which there is not enough.

As soon as man can compete for something, the thing becomes valuable to him. Supply is the prize and the value builds as man works to secure it. The more he is willing to put in for it or put up with other things so he can have it, the higher the value goes. The more effort, money, education and time he demonstrates to secure his prize, the more he dances with his shadow.

Tell a man a famine is coming and every grain of rice will become a nugget of gold. Show a man a storm is brewing or that a war is impending and he will look out and grab anything and everything in an attempt to secure an item of barter, a thing to trade, a talisman to keep him safe. It is a foolish wish. Behind the screen which mortal eyes perceive as that which separates man from his good, from his due, is just an empty mirror of desire for false things. He would be better off if they had remained invisible, for the moment he sees something of the material world, wants it, gets it, loses it, tries again, comes by it a second time, he is captured in a world that will do him in. It will exhaust him in his tail chasing and lie him down in the sleep of the doomed and it will not wake him until grace recognizes his willingness to stand up and be counted again.

Grace is the invisible option that you may bring into manifestation with no interference, and grace covers a lot of territory-all of it. Seek ye first the kingdom of heaven and all things will follow. There is no one who can divide grace. Greed, chance, manipulation and deception are nothing, reduced to ashes by the almighty power of its truth. Man cannot even put in a viable bid, for to mortal man grace is totally invisible. He is still out in the wilds of his vain thought, chasing supply that will meet his demand.

To the man who has learned to trust in the Lord, to that man will the unseen become visible. He will ride his rainbow right into heaven for only spiritual eyes discern true supply. God will be his sufficiency in all things, not what God gives him or makes him or shows him, just God being God. Anything else is merely an added thing. God himself is the sufficiency. Oh Lord, how long I have waited for you and how sweet the sound of your Presence. Time has disappeared into the infinite moment and right now, right here, you are my sweet, gentle song and the silver lining of my soul. "My fruit is better than gold, yea, than fine gold; and my revenue than choice silver. I lead in the way of righteous, in the midst of the paths of judgment. That I may cause those that love me to inherit substance; and I will fill their treasures. The Lord possessed me in the beginning of his way, before his works of old. I was set up from everlasting, from the beginning, or ever the earth was."[1]

11 *Who Says That You Cannot*

All may be quiet on the western front but have you kept watch on the eastern exposure. The light informs the horizon each new day and you must ever take leave of yesterday's shortcomings and integrate your lessons at daybreak.

Whoever told you yesterday that the limit was in effect must be taken to task again today. Search out this voice at first light for it whispers mistaken information into your ears the moment you arise. The limit of which he speaks is his own, locked in by the power of his belief, and he can only tell you his own limited experience. It is the only truth he knows and, poor one, it is not even the truth. Part company with this limited partner and turn to one who waits in greener pastures. "I know that thou canst do every thing, and that no thought can be withholden from thee."[1]

God is omnipotent. Nothing that you can conceive in spirit is beyond spirit's conception. Everything you conceive in spirit is welcomed into manifestation. This power will reach into your hands and remain there permanently if you use it with wisdom, love, patience and mercy, but most importantly, belief. Leave the mortal world of doubt that even in it holy vow of marriage believes "in sickness and in health." Even as two become one, the duality does not recognize the omnipotence of God.

This very day, take omnipotence into your sanctuary and let it take possession of your senses wherever thou goest. Look beyond the world that your eyes first see for that is the world out pictured by doubts, and focus behind the scenes where omnipotence has laid down the avenue of truth. Walk freely along its tracks. It bypasses every stop sign and renders meaningless every hint of caution.

Behold the geyser of possibilities that burst through all limits and gush toward heaven boiling with joy and steaming with passion. Inspiration will soak you through and through and you will be delivered on time to your divine rendezvous. "Return unto me, and I will return unto you, saith the Lord of hosts."[2]

12 *Seek Righteous Judgment*

There is much power in the simple act of doing the right thing. It requires discernment and courage but once the commitment is made, the power will be perpetual to the doer. The reason that man does not recognize this hallowed ground is because the right thing in man's vision is not the right thing in spirit's eyes.

Man has been taught right from wrong but has been educated in shades of gray. Thus, when it comes to action, things are not as black and white as his simple morality, and he is confounded. What was simple becomes overcome with infinite variety of interpretation and he becomes lost in his cloud of unknowing. If it were not so, he would not have a court system; it would not take a jury to decide a case, a judge to rule on justice.

To return to the simple act of doing the right thing, man must recognize the authoritative and controlling voice with which his mortal mind shouts into his ear. He must see that he has placed his trust in his conditioned brain, washed with false ideas of his elders from the time of his birth. He has not thought to question their truth or their wisdom and has no way to perceive their duplicity. As he grows into manhood and sees that he is deciding every case exclusively by tradition, he will realize that he has left no room for mercy. Tradition is a lovely tradition for surely God creates and blesses coats of many colors, but man must cast his individual vote toward perfection regardless of how captured he has been by his past. What was good will come forward with him. Truth lives on.

Once man overcomes the limits of tradition he must overcome the limits of his mind. Man's reason is not reasonable. It is a mere trick that he uses to settle things that are beyond the works of which he is capable. It reduces the sharpness of every hook so that he has a leg to stand on without humiliating himself altogether.

Man's reason claims itself impregnable, superior to all other claims that presume against it. It offers explanations in a language of such double talk that mankind merely accepts its power without question. He who appears most reasonable, subjugating his emotions and judgments most successfully behind the veiled curtain of arrogance, walks away with all the power. He makes the rules, decides the consequences. He makes the simple act of doing the right thing the most complex thing in the world.

Once man recognizes man's voice of reason as a clanging bell, he may hear instead the voice of God, "Come now, and let us reason together," says the Lord, "though your sins are like scarlet they shall be white as snow."[1] When the truth of righteous judgment informs man's spiritual ear, doing the right thing becomes the simple act it was meant to be. At the moment of decision, though one might wrestle for a moment to make sure he is using ears that hear, there will be no decision. The right thing will be thundered above the voice of elders, louder than man's clamor of reason. It will burst forth in consciousness.

God will show the right thing in such clarity that nothing will confound it. Only man's stubborn nature and the self righteousness of his traditions will block his perception. Nothing can overcome the all power of God. He has strewn the way with the natural light of discernment, understanding and mercy. All shades of gray will emerge from the shadows into perfect focus.

Man may gloriously impeach the unjust rulers and return to perform the simple act of doing the right thing. He will secure the freedom that comes with righteous judgment. No longer leaning into his own understanding, he will know the joy of the Lord in his every moment and in his every movement, now and forever. "Howbeit when he, the Spirit of truth, is come, he will guide you into all truth; for he shall not speak of himself; but whatsoever he shall hear, that shall he speak; and he will shew you things to come."[2]

As you learn not to judge but to seek righteous judgment, you become a guiding light in the world, for you will become of the elect whom others will turn to for truth. Having no agenda that is not for the purpose of serving God, God chooses you to become visible to those who are looking for heaven. As you extend your hand to a brother prodigal you will know the true meaning of life for there is no higher reward and no greater joy available to man than the joy that comes from recognizing and serving the will of the Lord.

13 *Your Holy Purpose*

Who you are this moment in the flesh is merely a token of who you are in the spiritual body. As you peel away more and more of the illusions that have colored your idea of reality, the truth will start to emerge. The Lord is not silent to those that seek him. Now is the appointed time when the vision shall speak.

You have been on a long journey. Most of it has been full of despair and disappointment. Every dream has gotten dashed. Every hope has lost its faith. Each painstaking step has yielded little territory. Nowhere does a sure thing seem to be in sight. Now, however, all these feelings of doom and gloom will reveal themselves as an essential part of the spiritual journey. Only despair allows one to look past what seems to be reality. Only disappointment leads one to consider an alternate route. Only lost hope shows man that he cannot find heaven in man and ultimately brings him to his knees.

It is time to look up from the third dimension and see it for what it is. It exists only as an entrance to life, only a lobby to the consciousness in which man will recognize the reason for his being. Nothing of man's first steps or early experiences are meant to be satisfying or fruitful. They cannot be for they are not intended for that purpose.

You have not failed. You have not made mistakes. You are not ignorant. Every day, from your entrance into the body until the moment of recognition, your every perception has been a building block on which your consciousness was being staged to emerge.

Your life differs in appearance from those of others because it is part of the plan. It forces you to notice differences, to place yourself somewhere on a continuum. It is grist for the mill that will grind you to perfection. While you are noticing that some lives seem harder than yours, while others appear easier, you pity and you envy. It is an experience common to everyone. Those whom you pity, pity others, and those whom you envy, envy others. Your life is not unique in human terms. Every human emotion you feel in your being is the same one all others feel. Every possible thought that can cross your mind will cross, at some time or other, every other mind. Even men whom you consider inferior have identical thoughts. They merely use a simpler vocabulary and less complex strategies. You are filled with no more or less doubt and fear than the next one.

Although you are like everyone else in human terms, your spiritual gifts are individual and are given you to use in service to God. As your consciousness recognizes that you are here for a holy purpose, that which is given you to do will become apparent. Whatever you are now doing may or may not be what the Lord has in mind for you but if it is, you will know it. There is no mistaking service. It is accompanied by a spiritual compulsion and causes you to investigate every possibility for bringing the work into expression. When the activity begins, regardless of the form it takes, you fall in love with it and find it natural, easy and fulfilling. It provides the answer to the meaning of your life which has ever been a human question. It teaches you the feeling of joy and gives you the distinct feeling that your life was all about arriving at this moment.

Service is not necessarily the work that you do. It is not defined by external description but by the vibration of joy in the body. There is a distinct feeling that you could spend every moment carrying out the activity and when you cease, you are drawn to return as soon as possible.

If you have not yet been shown your way, the Lord will reveal His will in good time. Or, perhaps, you are already an angel unaware, serving by the simple kind word to one who has lost the way. If so, you're home and God bless you.

14 *The Sacred Life*

There is no grander invitation you will ever receive than the invitation to the touch of the divine. You who are called have been given a supreme honor, the highest recognition that life offers to man.

It is time to take hold of the spiritual prize being held out to your receptivity, for you have journeyed far to discover its whereabouts and its substance.

Man has looked to death as his final hour. He has perceived life only as it takes place in the body and therefore has narrowed his ideas to fit between his physical birth and his physical passing. Consciousness is not so contained. It is synonymous with spirit which stretches life beyond time and space into the everlasting. This is where man must now recognize his destiny and restore his identity.

The fertile soil, which you have traveled bare back for so long, does not suddenly disappear at the edge of a precipice and throw you overboard into a grave. It flings you, you, to the altar of God and introduces you to the eternal life that lay just the other side of doubt, just below the deepest fear.

And what of this eternal life must you still accomplish in order to take its halo as your own?

If your time has come and you are ripe to harvest, you must cast aside every belief that is not of God. You must understand that there is no birth and death of you, no years that deliver you to the prime of your life and leave you for dead to be replaced by younger, newer flesh. There is no fortune with which you, as man, can purchase the pearl of great price, no beauty you can bring to match the light of its illumination. There is no intelligence with knows more than the all knowing God, no wisdom that is anything but foolishness in his almighty eyes. There is no land which you own which is of any value for the earth is the Lord's and the fullness thereof.

There is nothing to bring but your recognition for it is your recognition that instantly manifests the pearl into your safe keeping. Once there, you will never have another God before the one God. One God will protect his own. You will not need nor want, neither judge nor covet.

When the pearl of great price comes into your possession, it is yours to have and to hold. No earthly power can take it from you for it is invisible to mortal eyes and ears.

You will walk with your prize in freedom, spirit laying its way before your every step, guiding you to the ways of righteousness. The Lord will lift you above the trials and tribulations of man.

Welcome to the sacred life. It will prove you over and over again. All temptations of material reality will become transparent and their illusions will have no power to seduce you. Doubts will touch down into your vibration only to melt away at contact. Fear will come nigh your dwelling place and run away in terror as it glimpses itself in the mirror.

The Lord your God walks and talks with you in omnipresence, omnipotence and omniscience. Keep your mind and your heart stayed only on that which is holy. Regard not the world.

You are here in spiritual reality and no other place can sustain you for every other place is temporary at best. Life is everlasting. You are everlasting. God is the source who has breathed you into life, Who sees what he has created and has called you good.

REFERENCES

Page 103   1 I Samuel 3:9

Page 107   1 Psalms 48:10

Page 107   2 Psalms 24:1

Page 108   3 John 16:25

Page 110   1 Psalms 24:4-4

Page 113   1 Isaiah 55:81

Page 116   1 Ruth 1:16

Page 120   1 Proverbs 8:19-23

Page 121   1 Job 4:22

Page 122   2 Malachi 3:7

Page 123   1 Isaiah 1:18

Page 124   2 John 16:13

"Call unto me, and I will answer thee, and shew thee great and mighty things, which thou knowest not."

Jeremiah 33:3

"... prove me now herewith, saith the Lord of hosts, if I will not open you the windows of heaven, and pour you out a blessing, that there shall not be room enough to receive it."

Malachi 3:10

THE WAY
OF GRACE

BOOK V

TABLE OF CONTENTS

THE PREPARATION

Life does not meet the expectations that our mortal thoughts create. Outcomes that should have been so simple get held up by complexity. Things we thought would go our way demand another round of effort, another bit of time. We watch things fall apart that we were sure of and see things come together that were not how we had hoped. Little by little our sense of power and control slip away and we lose our way in confusion and disbelief. Even when we try again, having doctored our expectations more realistically, the outcomes still follow another rhyme, still respond to another reason.

The point comes when man's frustration drops him to his knees in hopelessness and humiliation. At best, although he turns a happy face to the world, he knows he has run out of options and optimism. He still holds his dreams but simply cannot seize them into his experience. It is a moment of man's darkest hour. It is also his finest. The way of grace does not appear until we admit defeat.

The Lord has said that his ways are not our ways, that his thoughts are not our thoughts. When the joys for which man is ever reaching are ever exceeding his grasp, the Lord's words start coming home to roost. This time we will be listening ...

1 *By A Way You Know Not Of*

The spiritual journey is the inevitable direction of man. He can only walk so far before realizing that he is gaining no ground, recognizing no reward. As he stops to see where he is, compared to where he thought he was going, a giant sense of his smallness grabs his gut. The arrest is made.

The commitments and contracts that man makes in the world of material reality hold him at the knife point of illusion. Only as he begins to perceive the great imitation of life's false treasures will he pierce the veil and get a look behind reality's door. He need only change goals. Fame and fortune are not the ultimate prizes; they are not prizes at all. They are merely dreams that grant him an audience with one eye while looking to fool the next one on line with the other. Even chance would give him better odds.

Fame is short lived by its very nature, a hot flash in the ever dimming limelight of man's worship of himself. Fortune is even more fickle. It misses the mark altogether, inflating and deflating in seconds, playing with man in proportion to the flimsy altar he has erected. No amount of fame or fortune will stay put in the human vault of security.

When man matures spiritually, be it at twenty six or ninety six, he learns that true fame rests in eyes that see and are seen of the Lord, that his fortune rests not in man but in God. The very moment he is willing to exchange the sword with which he seeks to conquer the world for the scepter of the Lord's will and testament, he will realize the inheritance to which he aspires. The prodigal son, the one who comes out from among the others, is a blessed man. He will be rich and famous for he has found the pearl of great price. Others talk gladly of giving everything they have for this pearl. It is only talk. They do no such thing. They create beautiful religions, erect splendid buildings and write profound scripture but they create only in the name of spirit, not in its works. Truth will get them in the end but, for the time being, patience has her perfect work.

You, my friend, are homeward bound. Having ears to hear, you have gained holy ground and will walk by a way the others know not. It is called the way of grace.

2 *Eternal Verities*

The eternal verities are the mark by which you may trace and synthesize all directions back to the point of origin. When you discover that the thoughts that you live by fail to match up to the world that they believe in, you may return from the mental north to the absolute truth from which you merely sidetracked into your own interpretation. God is absolute truth. Wherever or however you diminished his power by getting lost in your own image is found in the simple truth of the eternal verity that God is. With a mere touch of the truth, for truth must literally touch you, you will be assured that "Wither thou goest, I will go."[1]

From the south, where one has dipped the personality into the permanent ink of the shallow smile that masks doubt and fear, one may return to the birth gate of the new born. Arriving back to his spiritual origin, he may grow to spiritual maturity at a new address. Youth is wisdom's apprentice. One must first live life as if he ruled the universe before his many mistakes and lack of happiness make him receptive to wisdom's truth. And that it teaches is that God is and God is all that there is.

When "Be still and know that I am God ..."[2] awakens your consciousness to the presence of God, near you, for you, in you, as you, the falsity of world mind will have no place to convince you otherwise. Oil cannot capture nor contain water; once you have drunk at God's well, the oil will come out of your disbelief and be replaced by the cleansing, healing waters. For you, the eternal verities are back on line, revealing their single point of spiritual reality.

From the east, where false idols are born every day with another twenty four hours to impoverish you at the teller's window of material reality, you will be alchemized by a new centrifugal force. All that the Lord hath is thine. Look and recast your pearls in his honor. In the space of no time, those pearls will call forth the invaluable understanding of infinite supply. You will rotate on an axis that spins you in perfect rotation. God's power is the all and only power.

And from the west, where you reached your limit and could only see the setting sun disappear, the eternal verities will light up the understanding of eternal light. The sun is still shining, only your own eyes have misinterpreted the darkness as the absence of the sun and of the light. It is merely shining elsewhere from its everlasting orb to give you a moment to lie down, not a lifetime, not a death, just a moment to lie down so that the Lord may heal your flesh, freshen your dreams and lift your spirits. Not as thieves in the night come to steal your future but as knights in shining armor come to fulfill them do the eternal verities cause us to have light everlasting.

And from too high where your head spun around in dizzying circles in a desperate search for meaning and purpose, the eternal verities will ground you in the fertile soil of your own inner substance. The light headedness of too much air will be replaced with the solidity of your spirit, and harness you to a trustworthy relationship with your soul. The Lord starts from within before taking off in every direction to establish his dominion.

Just as God finished his seventh day in rest, you may rise from your descent to the underwater where you were drowning in the forgetfulness of flesh and sinking out of reach of memory of spirit. Now, peace be still once again, you may take a deep breath in spirit, buoyed by the Lord's love for you, and embrace the memory of who you are.

Arise in the morning to the eternal verities. Yesterday has given all it could. It has given you its pearls and as you start out in any direction with truth in hand and underfoot, you will meet up with yesterday in due time, due course, in perfect understanding.

All is one, one God, one time, one space, ever fixed, everlasting, ever peaceful. God sets his children back on course. As they traveled leaning on their own understanding and getting lost in its illusions, they forgot their point of origin and the source from whence they came.

The eternal verities stand as a statue of personal liberty, hand raised in salutation to the spirit of life within and crowned with recognition of the almighty God who shall ever be laying out the red carpet of grace before you.

3 *The High Way of Grace*

Along the way of grace one must meet every circumstance and condition with a moment of silence. It is this moment in which God reveals the nature of that which is appearing. A spiritual being lives to learn what lays behind the visible. Life has already shown him that things are not what they seem. If they are not, then what is it that is. The truth of things is given in that moment of silence.

Before one can hear information offered by spirit, one must first put his own reaction in check. All situations cause reaction. Quick judgment reels off its litany of possibilities. The body, ever faithful to the mind, comes quickly with its response. If the mind perceives a situation to be threatening, the body fills with fear. If the mind perceives a competitive situation, the body contracts, poised for battle.

The mind calls off shots as it sees them, off the top, devoid of confirmation or knowledge, lacking in discernment and wisdom. It merely follows a prescribed program of monkey see, monkey do with just a tad more sophistication. Perhaps ...

When the mind sizes up a situation as quickly as it sees it, it becomes stuck on a track and stays stuck as it continues along its well worn groove. It is the old record of things. This old record is what makes man old and commits him to a dead end.

If one would seize himself and take control of the runaway train of his mind, he would begin to perceive another world. Heaven cannot enter the consciousness of one who has already declared that all is lost. While the Lord is saying, Here I am, he is saying, where the hell am I. While the Lord is saying, I am the Lord thy God who brought you out of the land of bondage, he is asking, how the hell did I get here. Thus, one must work hard to remember that every situation will cause him to react and by this simple recognition open a window for himself. He will lift the needle off the old phonograph and make possible the music of the spheres. When he sees tears on a face he stops. Perhaps they are tears of unhappiness but perhaps they are tears of joy or relief or sand in the eye or the reaction to something very amusing.

It is a profound spiritual exercise to catch oneself in the act of falling prey to the persuasive information that one's eyes and ears see and hear. It is also the beginning of a new dimension of life, a higher consciousness in which one's vibration changes. This vibration has its own eyes and ears. With time and commitment to judge not, lest one be judged, one is poised to live in a new world where things truly are what they seem.

Circumstances do not shape your life. Your consciousness alters the circumstances to suit it. A tourist gets sunburned, a local gets tanned, a wise one stays out of the sun altogether.

One must stay true to the course to live a spirit led life. Although divine principles are absolute truth, they do not appear to one who is not looking. They provide perfect outcome only to those who live by them and who are in a position to recognize what a perfect outcome is.

You cannot play with divine principles or test them. They do not work on occasion, or manifest in the entertainment parlor. There is no reward or award that can touch or influence them. They are as they are, subject only to recognition and respect. With that, neutral and impersonal as they are, they wink a bit and shed their grace on thee. You, that is, you who have peeked around the corner and seen that heaven is, in deed, real ... after all. Each and every one.

4 *The Love of Grace, The Grace of Love*

Love is not easy. It is the reason why everyone seeks it but fears it as well. While love is new it is flattering to the senses. It purrs. Two hearts lay in the lap of luxury and drink up its miraculous milk. The mind cannot fathom that it has come into the love bed of such runaway bliss. All is well. Except all is not well. All is done in. As the passion plays out, one of the two will start insisting that the other is flawed.

The courtship quiver of love is not love. It is a physical attraction at the extreme end of the magnetic capacity to draw two together. Once the lock is made, it turns to possessiveness or repulsiveness in order to compensate for the loss of the individual integrity. It is over before it enters time. It is a flesh flood, a raging fire, a passionate note with no context to contain, maintain or sustain it. If every piano note was a passionate note, there would be no passion at all, just an overwhelming sound that reached a glorious crescendo for a moment before becoming indistinguishable, if not torturous.

Man is a spiritual being dressed in a body. One body may know another body but because neither perceives that they are not bodies at all, they love an illusion and emerge in the shadow of doubt. When the first bad breath of the morning glory dispels the spell, all is lost. That which is an illusion has no substance to feed it and must be revealed as the nothingness that illusion is.

Those who learn the truth of courtship and understand the urgency of its lessons are bound for glory. They have passed the first test of truth and will recognize the temptations of the world, smile, and walk on by. Those who do not, simply spot another butterfly and flutter their wings in yet another futile mating call.

The first and only thing that is true of love is that God is love and that his children, born of that love, are also love. Human love exists to stir our capacity to bring more of God's children to the world. It exists to raise our vibration so that we will remember our roots and our wings. Brought to our knees by the love of grace, we wake and are then gifted with the grace of love. The beloved is then understood to be one's spiritual companion, friend and lover, perfect as is. As Shakespeare said, "Love is not love which alters when it alterations finds."[1]

The moment one knows that love is given as a helpmate on the spiritual life journey, one looks to the other's spirit, not to the other's sins. Cupid's true arrow is not subject to physical laws of falling in or out of love, but to spiritual ones. Spiritual love enters time, picks up its passengers and lifts them on high, eternal unto the heavens. Love, lo and behold, is life's proof that I AM working in your life.

5 *The Substance of Grace*

The substance of a thing is all that matters. You get stuck with form only because it never occurs to the physical self to question what appears to it. Thus the eyes and ears cannot recognize a lie, even when it is staring them in the face. They see and hear only as they have been instructed to see and hear. They are form perceiving form, the kettle calling the kettle black.

The meaning of a thing is not the thing. The thing is only the letter of the alphabet which is merely pregnant with communication but not year capable of spelling it out to your comprehension. Until something touches your vision and opens it to understanding, you will know only the letter of things, not the spirit which moved the thing to come about. You will have your description and it will be perfect but it will be meaningless.

God is the substance of all things. He stands before you at all times, ready to reveal his presence at the moment your perception stops insisting on shape, size, color and price as the truth of what lay before you. It is a miraculous process to see the line of form disappearing and to begin to witness the reality standing behind the glass darkly. Your perception shifts in an instant, like looking at those black and white pictures in which one picture becomes the picture of something else when you look at the alternate color.

As you learn to discern substance from form, a reality long forgotten subtly becomes perceivable to your senses, not the physical ones but the awakening spiritual ones. Things you believed turn to emptiness as your eyes pierce the form and watch that there was nothing there but someone's belief that there was something there. You can put lines and circles together to form letters for an alphabet and you can choose five letters and make them spell d e a t h but you a living example of life, the substance of which can erase the letters with a few shakes of the wrist. "In the way of righteousness is life; and in the pathway thereof there is no death."[1]

As substance continues to overtake your old beliefs it will wipe the slate clean of the illusions appearing on the black-board of material reality. "It is written, Man shall not live by bread alone, but by every word that proceedeth out of the mouth of God."[2]

Substance is the deepest experience of life. It will lift you above form and introduce you to the strata of spirit. The new heaven and the new earth will remind your memory what it has stored within. The deep remembrance will cause you to breath a psalm of praise and gratitude that Home has declared itself to your memory. Your secret dreams will be revealed as dreams that are true. They mirror the only reality that ever was, is, will be or can be. All the goodness you prayed would be so, is so. You lost faith only because you were reared by those without it but you are never forsaken. When you venture out in your own consciousness with receptivity, your vision will be enlightened. The cloud of unknowing will drift away and, dear one, there you will stand.

Substance is the heart of every matter. It lays beneath the obvious and one sees it only as he looks behind face value. The world at large puts out its best case scenario and expects to draw a crowd. In this endeavor it is correct. Hungry souls respond to the false replica of things. Many a parent believed that wonder bread would improve their children in eight ways — the packaging and the words were that good.

Nothing has changed. Substance is available only to a few for they have held out for what's left after the others have consumed and filled up on promises and sales and left with tasteless ashes.

It is not a hard job to stay put while others are grabbing the goodies of mortal reality, once one has a few good experiences. It is a worthwhile endeavor to allow this experience to unfold in the present.

At the next opportunity, hold back from a hasty charge into purchasing something, believing something, deciding something. Take a stand and hold the stance. Hold it below visibility in the sub arena of your perspective. Substance is a true sub stance. It keeps you at bay while others are fighting to be first on line for anything or everything. Do not believe that you will lose your place. When the pickings are picked over, look and see that there is the very pearl you have always wanted. No one bought it or even bid on it for no one recognized it. What is yours waits and comes to you. Hold.

6 *Trust*

Young ones start out knowing nothing about trust. They simply trust. No reason has been given to introduce doubt. As the awareness of the world expands, the level of trust shrinks accordingly. Although some measure and memory of it is retained, mortality challenges the daily life experience with deceptive promises. The more one's needs and wishes are disregarded, the more one concludes that things are not trust worthy. They therefore double check everything in triplicate, thereby hoping to at least minimize the damage. Actually, they encourage it.

Before one can trust in God, one must rethink his relationship to others and realize that his lack of trust has stemmed more from his own reactions than from the behavior of another. A girl gets stood up on a date. She concludes that boys are not to be trusted. This is the natural response of the human to the environment. It is an incorrect response. Yet, as it stands, there is no human to break the chain and correct the links.

When one is hurt one must speak up, for to do otherwise is to martyr the self. The moment one speaks, the spell is broken, for one has claimed, as he must, his own self respect. No one can take away our respect without our permission. When one finds speaking up too difficult and opts to stew in private, he creates a misperception in his experience. This is an intense problem with society as a whole for in not teaching appropriate divine rebuke, it stores its reactions until the oil boils over in the pot and scalds everyone around. It sets suspicion into motion and suspicion is rotten. It corrodes trust.

You may begin again. Bite the bullet, don't shoot the gun. Do not make agreements idly, nor place your faith before it is justified. Do not respond to something because it looks good or jump in with both feet so that your exuberance fails to note the potholes and lands you in the landmine.

This thing you must do is called growing up. It is not related to years or age but to the understanding that each of us must move forward when we learn we are becoming cynical. Bitter people are only cynical people who never grew up, who preferred to place blame and leave it there. When one will not articulate one's displeasure, one has no room for forgiveness, mercy or understanding. One becomes brittle, hard, lost and unhappy. Old.

This is the day to turn the corner. Retract your conclusions and watch the outcomes upgrade to meet your maturity. The action of faith, not the words of it, cause the tree to fruit. Open your heart again and let it do your thinking. The mind will only judge everyone and everything out of existence, even one's own self cannot survive its overbearing tyranny. The heart sees, witnesses and understands. It knows the words and the actions that are perfect for every situation. While no human can change the human response, spirit can do anything. It lies ready to assist.

Remember this. You block your own way. No one can hold up the works when you declare you are moving forward. No one can say no when your spirit declares yes. No one can hurt you twice unless you agree to it a second time. Grow Up so that God may put things right. He will unhinge the resentments, clear up the misunderstanding. Let the other party go free and you will go free yourself.

You are not of this world. You are a link in a chain that binds not in slavery but in spirit. Let go of your hostage and let the spiritual principle of judge not, lest ye be judged move you spiritually. This is where you connect to God. This is the place where your trust is restored. When you speak your piece using courage and kindness, you speak your peace and it unfolds perfectly. Your needs and wishes may no longer be disregarded for you have placed them in the trustworthy hands of the Almighty who says unto you, "These are the things that ye shall do; Speak ye every man the truth to his neighbor; execute the judgment of truth and peace in your gates; And let none of you imagine evil in your hearts against his neighbor; and love no false oath: ..." [1]

7 *Understanding the Way of Grace*

You do not need an iron will on the way of grace, but a submissive one, because grace does the work you are appointed to do. Your effort of holding tight will only block its entrance. If you relax your grip, you will discover that the things you are fighting will relax theirs. The easiest way to accomplish this is to understand, yet once again, that every negative thought you entertain and every judgment you make, places blame on something or someone to whom it does not belong. It belongs to you. Mark this once again. It belongs to you and only you. If you were satisfied with the fullness of your own cup, you would not perceive that something out there rightfully belonged to you. You would be the one who could utter those holy words, forgive them, for they know not what they do.

Personal tension will begin to dissipate the moment you resume responsibility for your own consciousness. As you cease discharging random bits and pieces of blame, you become worthy. Although this may appear simplistic, you need only try it to see that it is so. The shortest distance between two spiritual points is no distance at all.

8 *Spiritual Health*

In the human world man feels very smart when he figures something out and watches the outcome work according to his calculations. The more challenging the problem, the prouder he feels to be the author of the solution. If he were to apply the same effort on behalf of divine principles he would really have something to shout about. This never occurs to him, however. His contentment comes from getting the quick fix, the one that adds up on paper. His discovery that one and one is two makes him feel like a hero, all puffed up on truth. His answers address principles of mortal reality, it's true, but they do not bring him one step closer to eternity.

Man is ecstatic when he discovers cures for disease. He does not realize another one will pop up to takes its place. One by one he conquers the new appearance, never taking disease itself, in any form, as the subject which should engage his attention. He continues to treat the body, when it is the soul that needs the work. If he were to treat for soul recognition he would not have to find a cure for disease. Health is a soul function. The body cannot reflect disease when there is nothing to reflect.

As simple as this is, mankind does not perceive it.

But you, reader, can accomplish it. You, reader, do not have to catch a cold. Next time a neighbor with a cold is nearby, remember that man's beliefs create his life and cause him to call things truth which are only truth for him. Turn the other cheek and look away from the idea of contagion. Let your neighbor have his own cold. The key is your consciousness, which is not simply words that you repeat such as I will not catch this cold, I will not catch this cold. That is voodoo, fear. That is not standing the high watch at the spiritual tower, that is total lack of faith, a demonstration that your belief is as casual as a toss of the coin. With a God like that, anyone would catch cold. No, your consciousness is a much safer haven, a simpler heaven than that. God is your health.

Into your understanding you must allow the idea that nothing springs into truth, truth is already present. It is never out of shape, out of form or different from the last time or the next time around. Nothing can diminish it or add to it no matter which way you come at it. A reaction in the body is a response to one's personal belief, the body itself is in fine shape. "And God said, Let us make man in our image, after our likeness ..."[1] When one is well "again", one has merely returned to the truth from which his beliefs detoured him. Nothing springs into truth. Truth springs into consciousness.

The easiest way to introduce health to the body is to recognize the negative effects of doubt. Doubt is a forceful power because it intrudes lightly and does not carry a big stick. It rather sneaks in to do its damage in tiny little increments of time, undetectably building a case. It snatches confidence by quiet erosion and keeps one off balance with its subtle presence. It throws you off your feet in an instant and never blinks its mortal eye. Doubt is a killer. You can, however, disarm it, before its weapon discharges in your body. Perhaps this is hard to understand but not if you truly think about it.

Doubt is the end of faith and the beginning of fear. It is a doorway whose door you can refuse to enter. Doubt says that there is a God, but maybe not. If you begin to see that doubt leaves no room for faith, you begin to recharge your vital,

God created, God maintained, God sustained body. There is no reason for sickness other than that it supports man's belief in it. Even doubt itself gives you a clue to its part in your undoing. Things will, without doubt, be better tomorrow.

We come to this world with life. When the Lord feels we're ready for the next one, we will go on. In the meantime we are here at his invitation, to carry out his will and to use time to perfect our understanding of divine principles. "Then shall thy light break forth as the morning, and thine health shall spring forth speedily; and thy righteousness shall go before thee; the glory of the Lord shall be thy reward." [2]

9 *The Power of Grace*

A moment comes on the spiritual path when you do, indeed, see God. All sense of separation disappears and the peace that passeth understanding passes to you. You can hear yourself shouting in gratitude, an inner shout, for it explodes within your heart. It is a secret, sacred and silent shout for the walls of Jericho come tumbling down to reveal the Promised Land.

All feelings of doubt are absent as the revelation unfolds, "… in quietness and in confidence shall be your strength …" [1] The experience of God replaces every question with a quickening vibration wherein lies the obvious answer. When the next mountain the Lord would have you climb appears, it no longer feels beyond climbing for your faith is automatically increased to match the ascent.

In God life, you will not love people less for their foolish ways but more, for you have just come from those foolish ways yourself. You do find, however, that you walk alone for most others still prefer their own ways, foolish or not.

Where do you end up when you give your consciousness over to spirit? You end Up. The thousand prickly, picky moments of doubt and fear that are forever holding you back fall away. Caution disappears, replaced by a certitude of no uncertain magnitude. Faltering and wavering no longer operate to throw your balance. The view point from on high reveals the ever present sense of God's presence. You no longer feel apart from your soul self for spirit closes the gap between mortal life and eternal life. You know what you are about. You are about your Father's business.

The power of grace to move you in its ways will direct your life in service to its will. At every turn, the complexities are worked out in advance so that the actions you must take appear simple and appealing. The sense of amazement and relief are ongoing as the burdens are lifted before they become too heavy. When Moses did not feel he could handle the peoples' faithlessness, even as they were fed manna in the wilderness, he appealed to God, "And the Lord said unto Moses, Gather unto me seventy men of the elders of Israel, whom thou knowest to be the elders of the people, and officers over them; and bring them unto the tabernacle of the congregation, that they may stand there with thee. And I will come down and talk with thee there; and I will take of the spirit which is upon thee, and will put it upon them; and they shall bear the burden of the people with thee, that thou bear it not thyself alone. [1]

Young ones of God, the ways of grace will carry you from henceforth and evermore. You have chosen a very Almighty God.

10 *Prayer of Grace, Grace of Prayer*

The way of grace starts with prayer. After that you need do nothing, for after that there is no thing. "... seek ye first the kingdom of God and his righteousness and all these things shall be added unto you."[1]

Prayer is a holy activity. It is a beginning and an end unto itself for it has a power that few have understood. As one plumbs its depths and sees that prayers are not pleading words spoken to a maybe so/maybe not God, one has the opportunity to rise to a deeper understanding.

Man has learned about prayer from other men but prayer does not answer to man but to his spirit. Thus, the wise seeker removes himself from the ways of his former teachers and teachings. The way of grace is unique, and unfolds by the One spirit to the individual who is brave enough to seek it out.

To undo the teaching of a lifetime that ancestors pass on through their laws and punishments is a daunting task. You must prepare for such an undertaking for such is the course of recognition.

The old does not automatically give way to the new. The old repeats itself time and again, appearing new, until one sees the illusion. The child repeats what it has learned and by the time its flesh has taken on the adult form, not a jot has changed except a date on a man made calendar.

Come out from among them and open to the way of grace. It can only touch those who prepare the way, those who are willing to forego the comfort of familiarity and the approval of their peers and elders. One must contemplate beyond the limits that teachers have set. The leader of a herd is not necessarily smarter than the others, just braver. He may lead the pack to physical safety but spirit has more to say about life "in the beginning." It goes on to evolve and to reveal life without end.

The difference happens when one suffers the tension to be so for just a little while as the new idea opens the eyes that have been pried shut by former belief. One next hears the definite declaration, "this is the way, walk ye in it."[2]

Prayer is the setting out a cup for Elijah, the opening of the holy door so that the Lord may enter and sup with you. You must not be mumbling words that will fill your ears with the sound of your own voice and that of your forefathers — the Lord speaks in silence. Be still.

11 *Graceful Patience*

Patience is the intimate activity of faith. Together they are the everlasting soul mates of spirit.

As man sees the promise of the things to come, he accepts the promise in lieu of the real thing. While he is responding to the glitter, his brother who has overcome the illusory world is walking down the road paved with gold. Man would forever be denied that which he seeks if patience did not come around to point the way.

Patience is the cure to the disease of the soul which is fear.

It is God's medicine. It is a strong anecdote, for fear is a powerful destroyer that enters the mind and seeps into the very bones and dries them up and cause them to rot and to appear to be no more.

What is patience? It is faith in action. As fear changes its nature so it may overtake you at will, patience is the sight that allows you to see beyond the fear to the outcome that will unfold on your behalf. No matter what is appearing, patience stands steadfast, disregarding the tricky deception with which fear seduces one who has no patience.

Patience is fertile soil, so fertile that it is the only place that grace will open its blossoms. To one who picks the flowers as they appear, there is no bouquet.

Man is so sure that he must hurry in order to take care of his own that he rushes out and about and trips all over himself, invariably coming up empty and apologizing for the shortfall. He places his sights on the next time. Next time never comes. He sets out still believing in the quick turn-around. He must beat the wolves before they run off with the goods. The faster something returns that he has put out to bid, the calmer he feels because his lack of trust gives him a perpetual feeling of tension and nervousness. He wants a thing signed, sealed and delivered at the moment he conceives it.

There is no faith in impatience, only fear. As a result the miracle is blocked from manifesting. Man cannot tell God about a date on the calendar by which God must perform. God's ways are not man's ways. God's ways are unlimited and mysterious, unperceived by man's sense of limited time, space and faith. As man insists on getting the matter over with, he hurries to his grave. At last, there he will have a dozen bouquets. Alas, his mortal eyes have closed and he will see them not.

One may cultivate patience but one cannot come by its majesty simply by the appearance of a bow. Patience is wiser than man, not fooled by his tricks nor taken in by his insincerity. Only as man surrenders himself does he begin to understand how he may come into its good graces.

These are the things patience reveals.

She must be in charge at all times. There can be no pleading for one's life, no begging for instant mercy. She is the one, the only one, who has no time to waste.

She will deliver only that which is authentic. Given time out from man's time, she replace man's impatience with wisdom to insure that the perfect solution will come about.

She does not always pay in ways one anticipates. Sometimes she will reveal a truth that is important to the future, the infinite future, rather than the immediate need. Her perspective keeps the eternal good, not the immediate goal, as her soul priority.

Patience is hard to come by for man. Although he would love to be a saint, he turns down the very means by which he might become one.

Patience has a distinct vibration that is unfamiliar to he who hurries. It requires him to trust in an outcome without controlling the factors that lead to it. A patient man is the only man in control.

The spiritual journey requires you to wear the apron of patience at all times for her work is not done until you see God, face to face.

12 *The Works of Grace*

Grace is simple eloquence, always ready to bestow gifts. Sacred, sensitive and perceptive, she does not appear to one who will disavow her beneficence.

One usually recognizes grace only after her works are accomplished. The more one comes to understand her ways, the more one will take no thought. The more one takes no thought the more grace appears. It is the peaceful and perfect equation of spirit.

As a child of God, you are always a child of God. At eight, eighteen or eighty eight, even as your body appears in the various ages and stages of man, you are ever the child of God and grace will ever be your godparent. You may give up the difficulty of life's hardness when you let yourself once again trust that what's yours will come to you.

Child of God, at this very moment become still. Step outside yourself for one moment and behold the burdens setting upon your shoulders, weighing you down with life's not so human ways. These burdens that you carry are not real. You are but a child and not meant to live in such hazardous consciousness. Let the Lord intervene and lift the weight caused by the belief in a lesser God.

Let grace come and envelop you with the answers, whereby your life returns to joy. Remember, you need take no thought. There is another way, the way of grace, and it will perfect that which concerns you.

Grace asks that you understand that it comes by a way

you know not of. You may not inform it, it informs you. Take no thought does not mean, however, take no action. Grace looks for those who are down on their knees. It comes to those living in faith, praying in silence.

If you are able to be still now, Grace, your godparent, who is looking your way kindly, will make an approach.

13 *Quickened*

On the way of grace a moment comes when every drop of faith one has demonstrated mixes with every other drop and results in a whole which is greater than the sum of its parts. Thus, every moment when you hold for God rather than man, may be the moment consciousness erupts. At this moment spirit breaks out into recognition and one sees that one is seen of the Lord. You will recognize this divine moment as the supreme moment of life. It will register its truth as an exquisite vibration you cannot mistake.

Having waited so long and pursued so many paths, it is startling to come upon your spiritual birth. In a moment yesterday is gone. The literal experience of life begins and you see how the entire preceding sense of time and circumstance were all a third dimensional part of the journey. Some experience this or talk about it as an NDE, near death experience. It is the opposite.

Here you are now. The burden is lifted. The empty cup has been passed to someone else whose faith is lacking but yours is overflowing. As your identity reveals the knowledge that I am present to you always, a sense of relaxation suffuses the body and permeates the mind. Alas, you give God's job back to God. You are no longer in the mortal hands of man but in the immortal arms of God.

14 *Change*

The way of grace demands that you remain open to change. God is always active in your environment, closer than you imagine. With your nose perpetually to the grindstone, you may miss the rewards of your labor.

Change need not be a threatening thing. The ways you have already perfected are yours forever. Truth gives them to you freely. It is the mortal ways that linger that you must submit to the hand of God so that He may perfect them. Increased understanding does not take anything from you; it multiplies your inheritance.

Wherever or whenever you feel doubt or fear, that is a moment where change is inevitable. Leftover from mortal man's lack of faith, they hold up unfoldment and growth.

Doubt and fear are themselves the problem. They feed on your willingness to entertain them. As you allow them time and space and free reign in your life, they continuously feed your imagination with whatever it takes to stay in control. They draw from everything happening about you so that they appear to be in the know. They will not give a moment's peace. They cannot, for they are your very enemies.

Doubt and fear have no substance. They are mere form. The moment you become open to change, their existence is threatened for while they are your mortal enemies, they have one too, change.

You need not make change for its own sake. You will be informed as you go. It is the openness that is important. Truth must have access at all times for until it is established, something must change.

When doubt and fear no longer have you in their grip, you will no longer need to think about change, for your consciousness will reveal the truth which is not subject to change. Where truth prevails, one experiences the presence of God. There is no room for anything else there but God and your recognition.

In the beginning, change is a difficult consideration, a challenging activity. Mortal man is very comfortable with the status quo. It makes him feel safe and in control. The very predictability of his routines gives him a sense of comfort and time. The familiar things around him assure that life is ongoing and will not leave him out of the loop. The thought of change interrupts his sense of time and its flow. He is afraid the past will jump back into his life and that the future will fall apart before his very eyes. The grindstone is a much more dependable touchstone to preserve his current sense of place.

When one who is called decides to heed the call, change is less threatening. The moment one allows himself the initial steps, he discovers that his life is intact and that he has survived the catastrophe that fear convinced him was real. Slowly the shadows that were filled with imaginary demons and goblins come into the light and he perceives that they were illusions of his mortal mind. Rather than fall prey to pain and death, which were his worst doubts and fears, he begins to discover a new lightness that comes from freedom.

As man slowly raises his nose from the mortal grind-stone, his vision takes in the world he could not formerly perceive. "And out of the ground made the Lord God to grow every tree that is pleasant to the sight, and good for food, the tree of life also in the midst of the garden, and the tree of knowledge of good and evil."[1] Aware that his unwillingness to change held him victim to fear doubt and fear, which were the only enemies, the only evil, he now turns to the tree of life for his sustenance.

15 *Prove Me Now*

The way of grace is an infinite way. It bypasses the detours, winds around the wrong turns and carries the child of God safely though the valley of the shadow of death.

One knows when he has arrived safety to life everlasting. He recognizes that he has moved from third dimensional reality in the shoes of mortal man to the next leg of the journey. The past, which once seemed so full of importance, takes on an illusory quality as if it only existed as a passage way to this moment, to this understanding, to this recognition.

Breathing changes in the fourth dimension. Heaven's breath is not a respiration in fear but in perfected faith. One's vibration, quickened beyond the limit of mortality, operates in harmonic flow with universal truth. One inhales recognition and exhales gratitude in a perpetual astonishment of the goodness of the Lord.

Consciousness is the dwelling place toward which human life has ever been leading. As it suffuses through one's life stream, it cleanses and carries away the notions of olde, leaving in its place the memory of spirit whose lifeblood is eternal.

This lifeblood, so full of richness and manna, places one in perpetual service to God's will so that there is a full bodied, permanent answer to the meaning and purpose of life. One's futile search for happiness abruptly ends as it crashes into the outbreak of overwhelming joy. This is an unmistakable experience, the welcome mat to the way of grace.

From this moment one takes no thought but gives all attention to listening. The initial sounds are disregarded. They are recognized as the voices of olde, trying to reclaim the one who has escaped so that they may flesh out their dead bones and justify their olde ways. As the ancestral heritage is overcome, the sounds of reality begin. Now does one understand the meaning of ears that hear, for now, at last, the pearl of great price reveals its value. The word of the Lord shall not return void. It sounds its presence in one that withstands and serves the truth. To him that hears, the Lord shall speak. Do you hear? The Lord will speak to you. You need not look away. There is not another. The Lord will speak with you. This is the way, walk ye in it. It is the way of grace. And you have chosen it and it has chosen you.

The way of grace receives you and on it you meet all life with the simple prayer, "Prove me now." The Lord's blessing will cover you from head to toe and go before you to accomplish its ends.

All things that would assail or assault will be dealt with on your behalf. All outcomes will emerge in divine order, no matter what density or darkness appears to impede it. The thunder and lightening of the Lord's omnipotence will come to the aid of one on the way of grace who has uttered, "Prove me now."

You, child of God, need weep no more. The way of grace has awaited your arrival and recognizes your footstep. Having left the ways of the world to bring yourself and your first fruits to the altar of the Almighty, you may walk on in peace, in joy, in love.

"Bring ye all the tithes into the storehouse, that there may be meat in mine house, and prove me now herewith, saith the Lord of hosts, if I will not open the windows of heaven and pour you out a blessing that there shall not be room enough to receive it."[1]

REFERENCES

Page 139   1   Ruth 1:16

Page 140   2   Psalms 46:10

Page 145   1   Sonnet 116

Page 147   1   Proverbs 12:28

Page 147   2   Matthew 4:4

Page 150   1   Zechariah 8:16-17

Page 153   1   Genesis 1:26

Page 154   2   Isaiah 58:8

Page 154   1   Isaiah 30:15

Page 155   1   Numbers 11:16-17

Page 156   1   Matthew 6:33

Page 157   2   Isaiah 30:21

Page 164   1   Genesis 2:9

Page 166   1   Malachi 3:10

"Know therefore this day, and consider it in thine heart, that the Lord he is God in heaven above, and upon the earth beneath; there is none else."

Deuteronomy 4:39

"Give ear, O ye heavens, and I will speak; and hear, O earth, the words of my mouth. My doctrine shall drop as the rain, my speech shall distil as the dew, as the small rain upon the tender herb, and as the showers upon the grass: Because I will publish the name of the Lord; ascribe ye greatness unto our God ..."

Deuteronomy 32:1-3

BE STILL
AND KNOW

BOOK VI

TABLE OF CONTENTS

THE CALL

The life of man carries him to many destinations, none of which he remembers choosing. When he regards the outcomes of his hopes and dreams and sees that even those he has achieved have brought little satisfaction and definitely no joy, he is at a loss. Although not yet ready to resign he does not know how to proceed.

This is an important moment. Having come this far, one at least knows that the road he is on dead ends. He has been here before, he is here again. This is the moment requiring and defining a leap of faith. This is the predestined place instilled in man to help him recognize and claim his soul.

One man is going to perceive anew. He will be assisted and guided by spirit for in choosing to follow the way of spirit, spirit will lead the way. This is the narrow road, the one that few there be that find it. It is not a familiar reality and none of its experiences result in the outcomes that man's reasoned out steps predict. This is a new way and here is where man will lose himself and find Himself. The joys that only spirit possesses, that only spirit distributes, are about to name his name, your name.

You are one who is going to hear the call and turn. The others will remain right where they are, as they are, perceiving as usual. You may find them at any time, for although you are taking a journey, you are not out of sight, nor out of reach, merely the rabbit in the tortoise and hare parable. Someday the others will be along, perhaps yet in this lifetime, but you, child of God, have been called and by your answer all things will be brought to your remembrance. Be still and know.

1 *The Veil of Stillness*

Man is a creature of habit. Take them away and he will restore them. Move him to a new place and he will create new ones. Force him to change one and he will become nervous. Insist that he break one and he'll hold on to it twice as hard or desperately search for substitutes. Failing that, he'll fall to pieces.

Habits give man the illusion that he can cope. They buy him time so that he may figure out how to maintain control. He exercises them automatically, without thought, and thus believes that he is safe, that nothing can happen until he says so. He is so habituated in going from one habit to another that the world could be crashing and he will be disinterested until he has had his morning coffee.

Habits are man's closest knit enemies. Rather than provide him an interval of rest in between the activities of a dynamic life, habits camouflage him in their perpetual sameness, hoping to escape notice until he himself feels like looking up, or out.

The moment comes when man has a rude awakening. While he was sleeping, tiptoeing from one habit to another, a whole world was occurring and he is out of touch, far behind in his capacity to perceive, to understand, to act or to accomplish a thing, except his own end. He has become putty to those around him who inform him what to believe, how to behave and what to think. While he was refusing to budge before the clock went off, whole governments formed who would send him and his sons off to war. Entire religions were created to tell him the whereabouts of his soul, and where and under what conditions he could buy it back.

Man holds on to his habits for dear life yet, all the while, they are blocking heaven from his reach, locking him this side of its riches. Although man, if asked, could name his own habits, he is unaware that the cost he pays to maintain them leaves him nothing to go on.

Habits are thick veils that retard man in his evolution. They are the covering over his eyes that cause him to see only the obvious, obscuring truth from his view. While man is using the valuable time he is given to relive the same moments over and over, which is what habits are, he becomes blind. Life everlasting is outside his perception for he is lost in the wrong time zone, fearful to lift the veil and behold his destiny.

Oh, man, peek out from the past and rest beside the quiet waters of stillness. Let your soul silently and sacredly come forth to stake its claim. It only wants to introduce itself to your recognition. You are not who you think you are; you are more than that, so much more, and in your heart you know this.

All over again is a place you can visit only so many times before you feel like a failure. You have not failed for lack of trying but for lack of understanding. Experience will fill the void.

When something is not working, you are being called to another way. A little trust and a little faith will go a long way but only if you choose a tree ripe to harvest. The juice from the old grapes is gone. There is new fruit, sweeter wine. It will mirror the precious inner hope that you really are a beloved of God, seen and cherished in His eyes. When you are ready, Spirit will reveal itself so that you will know this for sure.

2 *The Qualities of Stillness*

Stillness is a blessed state. It allows man the familiarity he craves without inducing sleep. It has an omnipresent quality so that man may access it as easily as he wants and as often.

Stillness exceeds the comfort of man's old habits for he will never be forced to give it up. Being a sacred and secret area within him, he may take flight or refuge as he wishes and remain totally anonymous.

Stillness maintains its own authority and submits only to its own jurisdiction. Having no enemy, man may go there safely and if, perchance, he looks over his shoulder, there will be no one there, could be no one there. The entry way to stillness permits only one to enter and then it seals itself into a sacred sanctum and becomes invisible.

Being a quiet activity, stillness provides man the peace for which he hungers. Habits offer him no peace. Based on fear they chase him from one hiding place to another, like a squirrel nervously checking each hole as a potential winter warehouse.

Stillness is an easy activity, made free flowing by its simplicity. There is no complexity to confound its whereabouts and no entrance requirements to hold up its works.

Stillness has no form and no limit and thus there is no exclusivity. Any man may partake according to his own need. Being an aspect and function of infinite supply, its quantity never reduces, regardless of the multitude that seek it.

Stillness takes place outside of time and space. It answers the moment it is called for there is no gravity or density to waylay its movement.

Although stillness has no appointment book or calendar, one must nonetheless make the decision on its behalf for it to manifest. As near as it always is, it is far from those who take life in the mortal realm of time, space and senses. Thus, the sooner one decides that that the moment is at hand, the sooner does the tree bring forth its tree yielding seed.

There is no lack of depth to which stillness will go to reveal what is asked of it and no height it cannot attain to lift one as high as one chooses to go.

Stillness is a gift of God. It is an engraved invitation addressed to man. Be still and know ...

3 *The Courage of Stillness*

Life offers its choices every day. It is not static but alive with consciousness. As man faces the days he has been given, he must decide his response to events as they occur. Either he will hand his problems over to doubt or he will hand them over to faith.

Those who have chosen doubt find life to be a perpetual exercise in fear. Their doubts become habits and they find a dozen new ones a day to offer to their God who has no remedy. They have chosen an idle idol which takes no account of man for it is man's very doubts that sustain their perpetual existence. You, however, no longer need to walk this way. You may emerge from your damned up hiding places. When you are no longer looking down, you will be looking up.

Stillness is a long way from the third dimension where your senses rule your perceptions and your perceptions rule your senses. When one's name is called in stillness, courage hears the sound. It releases one you from the stiff-necked beliefs of the ancestors who refused to hold their faith. To you, child of God, life will reveal its secrets. "But if from thence thou shalt seek the Lord thy God, thou shalt find him, if thou seek him with all thy heart and with all thy soul." [1] You do not need to find God, only to seek, for God is already present, subject only to your awareness.

Courage is the recognition that you need not wait to be perfect but to realize that perfection looks for an invitation to do its work. As your courage to refuse doubt becomes stronger, your doubts automatically become weaker. Without fuel they reveal themselves to be without substance, words without meaning. Doubts procreate only in their own image. Courage cuts off their power and one may proceed with undisturbed confidence. As one overcomes doubts, he breaks the habits that become their hiding place and thus eliminates the fear that they engender. In the stillness that follows, faith rears her new young ones. "Wait on the Lord; be of good courage, and he shall strengthen thine heart ..." [2]

4 *The Stillness of Stillness*

Until you get to the truth, everything has aspects. One man goes to another with his problems and the other man responds, "No problem." Each person has a "to do" list of things to overcome and a finished sheet of things he has mastered. Life is an ongoing attempt to take everything from column A and move it to column B. In the stillness of stillness another option emerges. Stillness has something to say.

Problems are created by man. This is a natural thing for him to do in the third dimension. His mind is not yet under his control. It places everything in duality and perceives everything in contrast. He does not know that he has this pattern; it is merely imprinted on him from those just before him in an endless display of mortal futility.

When man looks out and understands what he sees only in terms of contrast, he is forced to distinguish one thing from another by assigning qualities to each. While something is here, something else is there. If this is up, that must be down. One thing is hot, another cold. She is beautiful, that one's a toad. If comparison remained this simple, man would have no problem. Comparison, does not, however, stay static in man's thought but continues until he perceives every thing in pairs of opposites, inevitably seeing everything as for him or against him, as good or evil. Now he has set up a world in which he must share with the good and the evil. Thus he always feels only half way safe.

Having manifested a world view of good and evil, he must now protect himself from his perceived enemies. Once he was a child of God offered life in the Garden of Eden where the fruit from the tree of life and every green herb would sustain him until life everlasting. Now he sees an enemy and believes, like Cain, that his brother must go.

Once a man perceives an enemy, he himself becomes the enemy. In mortal eyes, that no longer immortalize, he sees only the mirror image of his own projection. He believes that good exists and that he must use his life to make room for it to spread and thereby justifies killing off those who are taking up its room.

Now would stillness tell you to be still and know. There is no good and evil. There are no pairs of opposites. The Lord created a perfect world, in his own image and the Lord is One.

Man, be still. Let Spirit show you a dimension beyond the third where you live, for if you live in a world where you perceive opposites, you must also die.

In the fourth dimension, pending your recognition, the enemy is just another false idol, another god who distracted you from seeing that the Lord is One. If thou hast another god before me, how shalt thou see Me?

Be still. There is no enemy out there, up there, down there. There are not two brothers; all men are brothers, equal in the eyes of eternity.

Only as a spiritual outcast did you see a mortal world reflect back a mortal man and thus were you deceived. Now, in the stillness of stillness, does the gift of the Garden of Eden reappear in all its splendor and there you are. You are the expression of the Lord's will, a reflection of his perfection. You are none other. In the stillness of stillness, there is only

God. There is only His life. You are its substance.

Go in peace and remain in stillness. The enemies you perceive will fall away for they are only illusions born of fear. As you keep your mind stayed on God you will learn that He does not forsake your brothers and He does not forsake you. In stillness, the dear and gentle life you long for will come in and lift you up. The only place you wanted to be is the place where you now arrive. The earth was conceived from heaven and its children born thereof. Heaven and earth are not two places but one and you are the one who brings them together.

5 *The Activity of Stillness*

Consciousness is the atmosphere of spirit. By its action, awareness occurs without the saying of words or the thinking of thoughts. It is the result without the effort. Skipping the perception of man who perceives inaccurately by relying on physical senses, consciousness reveals the perfection that is already present in him, as him.

Consciousness as an activity of stillness is a perpetual revelation. One who brings himself to the quiet, leaving behind his world of words and thoughts, becomes subject to the revelation. The spirit of the Lord informs the spirit of man as to the oneness and sameness of that spirit.

The more man submits his need to know to the activity of stillness, the more he will realize that he already knows. Nothing outside need be brought to his attention; that which is already within needs simply to be allowed recognition. Man was given his entire inheritance with the first breath which brought him to life.

Stillness is the most profound activity of time. It transforms man from creature to child, from lost to found. As he overcomes the initial self that was initiated in the third dimension and offers himself up to direct impartation, one moment he is still and the next he becomes a template for spiritual truth.

Revelation is the grand opening of the soul. Once one experiences this identity, he is closed to the ways of the world. The impartations of spirit do not come in part so that they must be put together to be figured out but are delivered directly to the comprehension. They do not have the capacity to fall apart, because, seamed in truth, there is no place where they may be diminished; no part exists to become unraveled. "The earth is the Lord's, and the fullness thereof; the world, and they that dwell therein."[1]

As one attends the opening ceremony of the new life of revelation, he begins to understand that this ceremony will be an ongoing celebration. The new life does not wear off and become old all over again. The fruitless, futile existence of repeating one's yesterdays disappears for good.

Life at sunrise is a new life. Man cannot know all there is to know but spirit does. Every dawning sheds new light, gives man a new name. Yesterday accomplishes nothing if it does not send man bravely forth into a new life each and every day.

6 *The Revelation of Stillness*

What is revelation? It is the revealing of the truth that precedes and exists outside man's beliefs, opinions, experience or training. It is unrelated to space and time and excludes all man made institutions including religions, governments, cultures and economic systems. It takes no account of age or gender, recognizes no concepts based on man's power of reason, and is oblivious to man's established laws.

Revelation is the natural order of things and has no beginning or end since change does not alter the truth from which it is derived. Man cannot come to revelation, revelation comes to man. Those to whom it comes are initiated into a brotherhood known as the elect. They do not need to stand up to be counted; the Lord has taken account of them.

The elect stand alone, existing outside the definition or limit of any group of any kind. Though called the brotherhood, the brothers need not know of each other in the flesh. They are linked only through a common understanding that there are others to whom revelation has been revealed.

The conduit of revelation and the depository of its substance is consciousness which does not increase or decrease with activity, merely opens its recipients to a perpetual possibility to deepen their comprehension of I am that I am.

Only as man voids the identity that he has given himself and recognizes his spiritual reality, does he create the opportunity to receive revelation. Only as he lives by the revelation he is shown will he be permitted to receive more. When he has surrendered totally to the process, he becomes illumined and the divine principal of life uses him as an instrument of its truth, as a communicator of its power.

Revelation is without bias or judgment. It is everyone's heritage, everyone's destiny. The consciousness of an individual determines how much he will receive and when. The more one surrenders his pride in personal power and recognizes that all accomplishment is made possible only from on High, the more he becomes a transparency through which revelation may conduct its expression. If he is willing, revelation is willing but revelation is wiser than man and won't cast pearls to the blind.

When you are sufficiently aware that mortal reality is merely illusion, a fancy shadow, revelation will scan you as a potential partner. If you live for anything else but to become a spiritual adept, you may not become one. Years or lifetimes later, however, you will find the way because revelation is truth and truth is the destiny of man, the will of God.

Now is the time to take your spiritually right full place. Give up your last ditch efforts to match life to your illusions. Lend an ear to life eternal lest the ditch becomes a grave and you have to take a long time out.

Revelation does not come to man but through man and, when it does, man knows that the human heart is moved by the hand of God and beats in perfect time with their mutual spirit. Witnessing the animation of life by its Creator brings man beyond time and back again so that he rises in consciousness. He has seen the future and there is no death.

Without the mortal tyranny of a life sandwiched between a regretful past and a shrinking future, man enters divine time and lives in a perpetual state of grace and gratitude. He beholds being held by God and there is nothing more to behold. The blessings start pouring and pouring and wash away all the fear that it might not be so ...

7 *The Substance of Stillness*

The Lord brings people out of bondage but people wander right back in. After the whooping and hollering are over, they long for the old ways and the familiar surroundings where they can justify their judgments and lack of faith.

All people start in bondage. It is the mortal way. One by one, each must decide if he will use this lifetime to come away from the Egypt of his own making, or remain with the group who has chosen to take life in yesteryear.

When one chooses freedom, he goes against everything he has ever been told, including the report which has come from his own eyes and ears. Instead, he turns to the still small voice that says there is another way, another world, follow Me.

The brave one who comes away must turn to the substance of stillness, Faith, to give him courage, for he cannot prove his point to the others. Having abandoned the thinking of the group, the support of the group abandons him. Fear not.

The brave one does not walk alone although it appears that there is no one at his side. The brotherhood of the elect makes a powerful statement within his inner ear.

Outside of Egypt, faith is the map. It is the walking cane that touches down on the highways and byways that are filled with the Lord's direction. The faithful one need not get scared and lost or run for cover. He has found the way home.

On man's journey to follow Me, faith is the spiritual food that will maintain and sustain him as he takes every step. Knowing that the world has already died, although there are people walking around in it, he "leans not unto his own understanding" but listens in stillness. He will never be forsaken or abandoned. His former family of man who continuously let the substance of stillness fade to gray, return one by one to Egypt. Perchance the faithful one meets one of these returning ones, he must keep the light on his own vision and a firm commitment in his step. He must permit no one, lest it be a dead man walking, to tell him where God lives or how to get to him. God himself is the revelator.

8 *The Reward of Stillness*

There is no reward that stillness will withhold assuming that one will not and does not mock God. Mortal man mocks God. He prays for tricks and treats that will make him feel good and look good. Even as his wishes are granted, his thank you is flip for he immediately puts in the next request. He cannot get enough of feeling good, looking good.

He who has learned that material reality itself mocks the material seeker, passes into a state of all that I have is thine. He has learned that it is spirit's pleasure to bestow on him every good thing. Spirit withholds nothing once it has found a true seeker. It gives freely that it might be known, experienced, enjoyed, reflected upon and passed on. Ask and ye shall receive is its motto, knock and it shall be opened unto you is its promise.

In the moment a reward is desired, a reward is prepared. Do not mock God, however. He will pick the moment. For you, time is always running out, moving inexorably to an end. For God, there is no time for eternity has swallowed it up. The gift will come to pass but not while you are waiting. You will simply become aware one day that it is so.

The rewards that are prepared in your spiritual name accompany you into life. All of the dreams you specifically dream are tied to their fulfillment and need only your consciousness to stir them into manifestation. As you grow beyond the gap that puts you in one place and your future in another, the distance meets and closes in the present. Future is only an illusionary thought that appears to the mortal mind that is not yet ready to make its claim. The spiritual one need not postpone anything. The one who becomes a doctor for the money and the status-for this one there is a future The one who is a healer, heals those around him in thought and deed in every breath he takes. When the title doctor is conferred, others give him the power to knit their broken bones. The healer knows, however, that it is always the broken heart that is bleeding and which must be healed. He therefore sets man back to Spirit. The body responds accordingly.

Let the reward of stillness open your eye to the blessings that this day brings. Do not be blind to them or feel unworthy of them or be too busy to believe that, yes, "This is the day which the Lord hath made; we will rejoice and be glad in it." [1]

As you recognize and count your blessings in each day, they will multiply by themselves. Do you see? Blessings are born in gratitude. They grow by recognition. They become infinite in consciousness.

Do not try to borrow from tomorrow and reap its blessing. There is nothing there. If you do not understand this, then there will be no blessings tomorrow or the day after that. Perchance you'll stop and enjoy what you call a moment of good luck but that will only confuse you because luck is inconsistent and arbitrary. It can only hold you back in the dark ages of your destiny. "Come now, says the Lord, let us reason together." [2] Do you see? In each day that you liken yourself in His image you receive the reward of stillness, the presence of God.

9 *The Rock of Stillness*

Actions speak louder than words but man's good intentions are backed by inattention, making him the author of empty promises. The Lord, being One, knows no such duplicity. His word is fulfilled from the spirit to the letter. The exact nature of the difference is measured by your own soul's resonance. It is either filled with joy or is always wanting, ever wishing, inevitably waiting ...

To get from no where to right there requires merely a moment, the precise moment that one makes a definite commitment to God. This definite moment should be so loud that is deafens man's old ways and blasts them to kingdom come.

Definite is the defining word for it is the definite commitment to God that defines the power to bring about the outcome. Behold!

Come ye now and do it. Let it go. Give it up. Toss it out. Leave "nothing" behind, the halfway measures, the "has been" habits. Search your bones and marrow for the last vestiges of excuses and alibis. Get past them. Get them past you. Delete.

Make a definite commitment to God and don't look back and watch if the Lord won't pour out a blessing and move mountains and cause there to let there be light.

God is all there is, just as the name promises. The word and the action are one. It is definite. It therefore recognizes only the definite. The rest is extraneous, empty, poof!

Make a definite commitment. Define it for yourself. Be precise that you do not waver. Sleep with it, eat it, live in it. Have eyes for none else. Make your commitment and mark your word. Sweep out the heathen that punctures faith with doubts. Turn the cheek quickly from the world of man. Wipe out appearances, here, now, with sudden and swift action.

Your definite commitment is the daybed of your destiny. Be still and watch Providence move with you. You shall wake and rise to see "all manner of unforeseen incidents and meetings and material assistance which no man could have dreamed would have come his way." [1]

The space between you and the Lord is now null and void, erased by your commitment. Behold, the Lord has come and "his reward is with him ...[2] The reward Is Him.

10 *The Mercy of Stillness*

Man has been taught to whistle a happy tune whenever he feels afraid. He cannot whistle that long. Putting on a happy face to grin and bear things that are unbearable is a false solution which only confounds the problem.

God is merciful. Man is not. As a result of man's inexperience with mercy, he doesn't know what it feels like or looks like. Although he has indeed heard about it, he prays instead for a lucky break and enough fortitude to get through his misery because he can't stand "it" any more.

Mercy is a natural reality to a man who attains a spiritual foothold on earth. His faith is his happy tune. While he is humming it, the Lord is perfecting the things that concern him. Having learned that the outcome of every situation is assuredly in his favor, he turns his impatience to prayerfulness and gratitude. He knows he is not alone and remains steadfastly aware that any assumption limits recognition. A man gets on a bus and sees a boy with one shoe. "Oh, I see you have lost a shoe!" "No, Mister, I found one."

If you will replace your negative reactions to life and place your attitude at a higher altitude, the release of stillness will consistently come to free you. It will deactivate the things that hurt you. You cannot get out of the way of a car unless you see it coming. When you open your spiritual eyes, the red lights/green lights of life will speak dramatically to your receptive consciousness. They will cause you to realize how to avoid man's ways which cause him only toil and trouble. The flashing red light will help you recognize the way not to go; the flashing green will take you to paradise.

A spiritual man is supremely blessed. Things do not go his way by chance. The spirit of the Lord is truly upon him. The moment he relaxes, closes his mortal eyes and opens his spiritual ones, he sees that his problems are gone. What does it matter that the other guy gets the bigger end of the stick. He can only whittle it down to nothing while he is singing his falsely happy tune. You, on the other hand, have gained the kingdom for God is indivisible, individually visible to his children.

Now, brother, this moment, lift the lid of the lockbox that has taken stronghold of your life and filled it with deprivation and dilemma. The mercy of the Lord is free. He will release you but first you must turn in earnest to his presence. In earnest is where you find Him. He will recognize you when you remove the false smile and the "make" believe words and actions. He will come to you, his own, and release you once, twice, a million times, whenever you are ready. The Lord's mercy comes with your life and endures unto all generations, unto all men. You are all generations and all men for time is eternity and you are the only begotten son.

11   *The How of Stillness*

Show me. Show me. Man's demand for proof has been unremitting. He has searched 'the world over', the only place where God is not for God is not of this world but of spirit. Only as one ceases to insist that his senses show him proof, does he stand ready to witness.

One finds God when one beseeches God himself to show Me. As he surrenders the form in which the evidence he requires must fit, he extends his first sincere invitation to be shown what he wishes to see. Man doe not so much seek to see God but to experience the miracles that are the substance of God's almighty reputation.

God proves man. Man proves God. In the spiritual realm, information is transmitted as a vibration of knowing. It reveals itself outside the process of thought and thus appears unattended by doubt. It wells up in its entirety with unmistakable sureness.

When one permits God to work in one's life, lets go and truly permits it, the outcome is perceived before and regardless of the facts. One watches the truth reveal itself, oblivious to all challenges. Any evidence to the contrary, no matter how real it appears, evaporates. Error must disappear. It is spiritual law. Over and over, through the outcome of every situation, one will see God. It is through the outcome that proof is finalized. The signs follow, they do not precede.

When one is touched by the first few "proofs," the ones that lead him further on the path, he begins to see that it is not the miracle that is miraculous but his seeing of it. It becomes an awesome "eye opening" understanding, minus thought, that the miracle is ever occurring, always occurring, and it is he who has been blind to it. While he was busy searching the world over with his eyes closed, his journey was futile. Now he begins his journey in reality and God himself will evidence his own reality. Man will be able to predict outcomes, without guessing, without reason or reasons, because he sees that the signs follow only when he allows God and only God to show the way.

God is revealed through the spiritual instincts that rise up to replace the physical ones that possess man. God will show Me in every moment. Life will become one coincidence after another until it is spiritually discerned that no coincidence is presence at all, the power of God doeth the works. While spiritual instincts are renovating the consciousness, spiritual sense begins to replace physical sense. One's eyes and ears automatically dismiss information in favor of the impressions, intuition and vision that emerge from within. They tell him what's what and what's not and inform him of the ways that he should go. When he is hungry, the fruit appears. It is always ripe for harvest.

Spiritual instinct and spiritual sense reveal that nothing is far fetched but up close, nearer than the eyes and ears, and faster. The one in a million will continuously pop into one's life. The beachcomber finds the heart shaped shell, the musician "hears" a new combination of notes, the writer the transforming phrase. Chance gives way to choice, stress relaxes into peace, doubts lose their power to create fear. Stay close to Me, and I will show you no fear. You do not need to get down on your knees but to never get up from them. You do not need to search. I am here and I will reveal my Self to your Self and you will be shown that we are one Self. Leave behind the old notion of Me. You can have Me only if you take Me as I Am.

12 *The Power of Stillness*

Man loves power, that which makes another subservient to his will. He perceives that the more he has, the fewer remain who can hurt him. This is the consciousness of mortal man.

In power, man feels like his soul has been glorified, that his mind has been given a higher purpose and his person a more exalted station. He uses his life and his lifetime in meaningless pursuit of the most advantageous place in the pecking order of his illusions. He feels assured that he is better than whoever comes next.

Power is the downfall of man. Even power over one other is too much power. It will delay the experience of heaven instantly.

Power is a cover. It spreads a blanket of illusion between he who appears to have it and he who appears to be subject to it. It covers up and redirects the other's attention away from one's laziness and insecurities, one's shame and fear. In essence, man's power has no essence. It is not capable of accomplishment. Being all show it has form but no substance. Power has no power. Why would man need power over another once he has achieved power over himself. And how would man achieve power over himself until he acknowledged that there was a Power higher than himself. Power is powerful only at the source, not at the effect. God is the source, the Cause of the effect. Man must become the very thing he demands of others to gain that which he seeks. He must become the subservient one. Thus, until he achieves this understanding, his very quest for power drives it further from his conquest. He will follow himself to the grave.

On the day you look in the mirror and know that you are not one with whom you see there but one with Whom you do not yet see there, you will realize power. On that day you are given your power for the Lord knows you will use it to serve not your own will, but His.

13 *The Surrender of Stillness*

It is rather simple to issue commands. It gets complex when the appropriate response does not automatically respond to its authority. The distance between thou shalt and man's response goes around the mortal world a thousand times a day without being heard. Told to be still, man responds as if he had been told to get a move on.

When man says, Lord, be Thee ever closer to me, his actions say, but first I must attend to my life. He then turns to medication or mediation to solve his problems as if meditation was not even in the realm of possibilities.

Be still is not only in the realm of possibilities, it is the only possibility. It is the meditation that brings the satisfaction of man's needs and desires to his experience. Only when the Lord says, let there be light, does the light so shine.

Now is the time to make a quick right turn for in the turning, the music of the spheres will sound a note. The resistance which plagues man with the inability to rise to a higher place will be dissolved by a higher vibration, breaking down his former self with tender mercy.

When all is said and done, it's just the beginning.

At last the moment of understanding breaks through man's oblivion and lights up his soul. Past errors are lifted above memory. Washed clean of confusion, man witnesses his place in God's plan for him and recognizes that he has arrived back at the beginning, all shiny and new. He has discovered the pearl of great price, his spiritual identity. The profound is profound not because it is complex and intrigues the mind but because it is simple and opens the heart.

To know is to have no doubts, for knowing is beyond thoughts and leaves no possibility for thought's process of reasoning to arrive at a vain or fearful conclusion. All outcomes are spiritual outcomes. Stillness equips man with the foresight of these outcomes before time brings them about and thus he no longer must wonder where he is going or what awaits him. He knows, now and forever, that his spirit is his reality and that his life is the will of God. He goes forth on a higher plane of existence.

All contemplation will be answered before the question is even asked. No sooner does he get ahead of himself than spirit brings him back to the moment in full remembrance that truth is always and in all ways the only answer.

Asked by his fellow monk why he carried the woman across the river when it was against the monastery's rules, the monk who saved the lady from distress replied, "I put her down on the other side of the river. Why are you still carrying her?" Rules are made for the man who needs a rule to tell him what is right. Those living in the spirit already know what is right and behave accordingly. When they hear, Be Still, in an instant they are on their knees to listen. No mortal rule can part man from God or God from his child. As soon as one is ready to surrender, the union is accomplished and the child of God becomes a visionary. He sees that truth is always the same, always reveals itself and always dictates the outcome. He goes forth in freedom for he is now in possession of the Pattern.

14 *Be Still*

Stillness signifies that man has overcome the mortality of reality. It is evidence that man has emptied his mind of its historic illusions and entered the time of all things shall be made new.

Life begins in stillness which is also known as divine time. One can only utter I see, I see, as heaven breaks through on earth into the moment of one's risen consciousness. Like a puppy shaking off water from its first bath and making a quick getaway to recover, man casts off the illusions that have hidden his spirit and shakes off the ordeal he has suffered in mortal limitation. He awakes to glory, glory hallelujah as his understanding displaces his fear, as revelation bursts higher than his mortal IQ.

And what of this side of stillness? What life is this new life? It is life everlasting. When death is no more, man moves in response to spirit. Perceptions become one with the truth of things and illusions of the world are constantly realized and dismissed as unreal. Each thought from the human past is overcome word for word as sounds of the divine peal through the consciousness ... and to you they shall be for food.

Mystery is the inability to see behind the glass darkly. An awoken spirit knows no mystery for it lives in light. The flesh and its senses, healed by the understanding that has dawned upon it, returns to Well Being. Trust is restored, for the memory of one's Self is brought to the remembrance and invalidates all man's former beliefs.

In stillness, no testaments cause a spirit to quake until the Lord has declared it to be so. Man's evidence is false and convinces him not otherwise.

Vibration moves within the flesh and reports to the senses. The senses of man's flesh, when replaced by spirit sense, report that all things are good and that one is protected moment to moment by his consciousness of God. No one may move upon the face of the waters but the spirit of God.

Peace is the natural equilibrium of stillness and stillness is a vibration that responds only when the Lord touches one of its strings to call forth spirit to its will. Thus, one lives in daily recognition that signs shall appear when the Lord is calling and until then he need take no thought.

The experience of stillness detaches man from his habits and history. It leaves spirit free on earth as it is in heaven so that it matters not where it is or whether it is in the body or not. Consciousness overrides to lo here, lo there, lo everywhere. Stillness feels. It feels wise and strong and safe. It feels powerful and full. It feels known, seen and understood. It feels blessed and everlasting. It feels joy. It feels God and God feels good. Be still ...

As man RSVPs to the engraved invitation that God addressed to him, he comes to know himself. He perceives at last, his life as God reflected, light to light, inseparable, one and the same, the one and only.

15 *And Know*

All good things must come to an end is only true in man's world. In spiritual reality all things are good and all good things are never ending. When you surrender your old belief to the ever lasting truth of God, your soul is freed from limitation of any kind. Men die for such a freedom but they think they can storm heaven by killing bodies. Mortal history knows better. Man is merely delivered from one extreme to the other, win/lose, good/evil, bounced back and forth as a pawn in an illusionary life peopled by men in search of power.

Be still and know has come to sweep you out of the world of lifelessness and helplessness, of lost hope and resignation. It delivers you a new life where your inner life is your only life. You are not a body that has taken on a spirit. You are a spirit that has taken on a body. Things that resonate in your heart, revealing the things you wish were true, come to pass as your daily bread. Every last morsel of hope leavens itself into manifestation. Faith is justified to such an infinite degree that if one should lose it for a moment, the next moment will restore it and deepen it.

The password of life is God. It will open any and every door. Go forth in His exclusive company for the Lord is the perfect escort and He alone is heaven.

There is but one step between you and life everlasting, between your birth and your joy, between your breath and your blessing. It is Be Still and Know.

Be Still and Know is an absolute. It is the one and only truth. It is spiritual grace and spiritual law. It recognizes every living being as its beloved.

This is the moment to forsake the world and to live only by the word of God. Take occupancy in your spiritual body and use only your spiritual knowledge to guide you.

Reach out your hand to heaven and heaven will answer with a mighty grip. It will lift you and carry you and uphold you forevermore.

Blessings to you on this holy day of your everlasting journey. "May the Lord bless thee, and keep thee; The Lord make his face to shine upon thee, and be gracious unto thee; The Lord lift up his countenance upon thee, and give thee peace."[1]

REFERENCES

Page 178 1 Deuteronomy 4:29

Page 178 2 Psalms 27:14

Page 182 1 Psalms 24:1

Page 187 1 Psalms 118:24

Page 188 2 Isaiah 1:18

Page 189 1 W.H. Murray

Page 189 2 Isaiah 40:10

Page 200 1 Numbers 6:24-26

If you have found comfort and recognition in this book and would like to read this author further, you may subscribe to her monthly newsletter, "The Divine Times." Subscriptions are $5 a month with a four month minimum.

Write: The Divine Times

973 Apokula Place

Kailua, Hawaii 96734

maramarin1@msn.com